THE WISDOM WHEEL OF INTEGRITY
COMPANION WORKBOOK TO THE ONLINE COURSE

seenson,
colour
element,
animal

Rosy Aronson, PhD

Seal Pup
PRESS
Berkeley, CA

The Wisdom Wheel of Integrity Companion Workbook
Part of the *Wisdom Keepers Oracle Deck Online Course Series*
Copyright © 2020 by Rosy Aronson
All rights reserved.

For permission requests, write to the publisher, addressed "Attention: Permissions Coordinator," at the address below.

Seal Pup Press
PO Box 138 Berkeley, CA 94701
sealpuppress.com
Writing and design by Rosy Aronson
Cover design by Rosy Aronson
Muse Consulting and Editing by Pam DeLeo, LMT

Ordering Information: **wisdomkeepers.net/SHOP**

The corresponding Online Course is available at: **wisdom-keepers.teachable.com**
For a special discount on Teachable, use coupon code: BOOK-OWNER

wisdomkeepers.net

ISBN: 978-1-7345848-3-7

Also by Rosy Aronson

The Wisdom Wheel of Integrity Online Course

The Wisdom Keepers Oracle Deck (Full color and B&W limited edition)

The Wisdom Keepers Inner Guidebook (Paperback & e-book editions)

Walking a Fine Line: How to Be a Professional Wisdom Keeper in the Healing Arts
(Online Course, Paperback & e-book editions)

64 Faces of Awakening (Artwork)

The 64 Faces of Awakening Coloring Book

64 Faces Projects (Global Outreach)

Designed to Blossom (Foundational Course and Creative Workbook in Human Design)

Designed to Blossom (Resource Book)

A Tale of Serendipity (Part One of the Wisdom Keepers Adventure Tales Series)

Dedicated to all who have dared to stand for Love in the face of Fear.

WISDOM KEEPING WORDS TO BEGIN OUR JOURNEY

Erica Gagnon, Canadian Artist & Ceremonial Leader

"These are important and historic times … as we are forced to realize how truly interconnected we all are here, together on this giant ball of earth, fire, water and air, floating in the middle of the Cosmos…

I encourage you to remain calm and to be kind and gentle with yourself and others … reminding you that in every crisis lie great teachings and gifts for us all.

Reminding you that you are your greatest healer, and to continue to transform and transmute any discordant and destructive energies with more love, more gratitude, more forgiveness and more compassion…

Reminding you that you are here for a reason … you were born for these times … with your gifts to share in the service of unconditional love for yourself, humanity, all beings and this Earth…

Let us reexamine our lives, our beliefs and our goals, and guide ourselves and our communities towards a new vision and a new reality of human existence upon this planet…"

CONTENTS

WELCOME!

I am so excited to be exploring the theme of *Integrity* with you. It is one that I have been grappling with for a long while. If you're here, my guess is that you have too.

The times that we are living in are so intense. I find myself, and so many of my clients, friends, colleagues, even mentors, moving from states of terror to excitement, from despair, to hope, to powerlessness, to empowerment, to emotional devastation, to evolutionary trust, to a painful sense of isolation and division, to a profound experience of communion and interconnectedness.

During extremely charged, and in many ways frightening times, it's easy to become derailed and lose our center. Many of us find ourselves getting lost in a frantic battle for survival and justice, or checking out completely in the guise of spirituality.

This is why I feel called to focus on *Integrity*, and to dive into this theme together with you through the **Wisdom Wheel of Integrity Online Course** as well as this **Companion Workbook**.

WHAT DOES *INTEGRITY* MEAN?

I looked up *Integrity* in the dictionary and found two definitions:

The quality of being honest and having strong moral principles; moral uprightness.

The state of being whole and undivided.

Together they create a beautiful paradox, one that the *Wisdom Keepers* are especially qualified to teach us how to hold, and walk.

WHEN WE ARE LIVING IN *INTEGRITY*...

… we are both soft and strong, receptive and dynamic, humble and assertive.

… we are able to take a stand for what and who we care about, without closing our hearts down to those who think or feel differently from us.

… we are able to clearly see the unfortunate consequences of "us vs. them" thinking and survival-based reactivity without getting swept up by the strong currents of our own judging minds.

… we are able to tell the difference between a grounded embodiment of our deepest spiritual values and a feel-good spiritual bypass.

… we are much better able to help others live in their *Integrity*, because we're not imposing our way on them.

BUT HOW DO WE GET THERE?
ESPECIALLY DURING SUCH DESTABILIZING TIMES?

When I'm tempted to check out or freak out, I call in the *Wisdom Keepers*. Even though you might say I created these beings, I actually consider myself to be their humble student. So, whenever I hear someone say that the *Wisdom Keepers* have become their friends, guides and family members, I totally relate!

In this course, we'll all be going on a journey together. Each of us—myself included—will be working with our own deck and calling in a unique Council of *Wisdom Keepers*.

While I will be calling in *Wisdom Keepers* to shed light on collective themes around *Integrity*, you will be calling in five *Wisdom Keepers*. They will take their rightful place in your *Wisdom Wheel* and help you uncover your unique way of understanding and expressing *Integrity* in your life.

Each *Wisdom Keeping* member of your Council will stand for an essential aspect of *Integrity*—**Loving-Kindness**, **Healthy Self-Respect**, **Courageous Self-Trust** and **Reverent Surrender**.

Before we get going, let me tell you what you're going to need to get the most out of this course. And then I'll give you a brief overview of the course's six modules.

WHAT YOU'RE GOING TO NEED

In addition to purchasing this Workbook and/or signing up for the **Wisdom Wheel of Integrity Online Course**, the most important thing you'll need is a *Wisdom Keepers Oracle Deck*. You can find instructions for ordering the deck on my website (**wisdomkeepers.net/SHOP**). I also encourage you to check out the **International Resellers** and **Stores** pages on my website as well, just in case there happen to be available decks in your neck of the woods!

If all else fails, contact me through my website, and you can purchase your deck through me.

The *Wisdom Keepers Oracle Deck* comes with a complete mini-*Inner Guidebook*.

If, however, you prefer a larger font size when reading, consider getting the larger paperback (or e-book) version of the *Wisdom Keepers Inner Guidebook* in addition to your *Oracle Deck*.

Paperback version of the *Wisdom Keepers Inner Guidebook*

NEW DEVELOPMENTS: I happily anticipate that the paperback (and some e-book versions) of the *Inner Guidebook* will be available in more languages (**wisdomkeepers.net/translators**).

OTHER THINGS YOU'RE GOING TO NEED

- a journal to write in
- a large sheet of paper
- a special place in your home or office that you've prepared especially for your **Wisdom Wheel**. Ideally, you can keep your Wheel out and available to you throughout the duration of the course.
- colored pens/markers/pencils, whatever you prefer
- either a cloth that you can use as a backdrop for your **Wisdom Wheel**, or a piece of paper with a large circle that you've drawn on it.

For a more complete experience, consider signing up for the **Wisdom Wheel of Integrity Online Course**. While much of the content from the Online Course can be found in this workbook, the Online Course is full of lovingly crafted and illustrative videos and more opportunities to interact.

You can learn about and sign up for the course here:

WISDOMKEEPERS.NET/INTEGRITY

Finally, I invite you to consider going through this process with a friend or a small group of trusted people. Whether you gather in person or via Zoom or Skype, set up a meeting schedule that works for everyone. Make sure that everyone has their own *Oracle Deck* to work with and that each person has their own workbook or has signed up for the Online Course, so they have access to the material and can fully participate from home. ENJOY!

A BRIEF OVERVIEW

INITIATION

In this first Module, we'll be:

- sharing the story behind the *Wisdom Keepers*
- introducing you to your own *Oracle Deck*
- helping you prepare your **Personal Wisdom Wheel** for the journey
- inviting you to choose the *Wisdom Keeper* who will be sitting at the heart of your **Personal Wisdom Wheel**
- initiating our journey together by choosing a *Wisdom Keeper* to sit at the heart of our **Collective Wisdom Wheel**
- offering practical suggestions for individuals, pairs and groups to explore further.

LOVING-KINDNESS

In the second Module, we'll be:

- exploring the Council Seat of *Loving-Kindness*
- getting to know the *Wisdom Keeper* who's come to support us on a Collective level
- calling in the specific *Wisdom Keeper* who's meant to sit in the seat of *Loving-Kindness* in your **Personal Wisdom Wheel**
- receiving practical invitations to explore *Loving-Kindness* more deeply on your own and/or with others.

HEALTHY SELF-RESPECT

In the third Module, we'll be:

- exploring the Council Seat of *Healthy Self-Respect*
- getting to know the *Wisdom Keeper* who's come to support us on a Collective level
- calling in the specific *Wisdom Keeper* who's meant to sit in the seat of *Healthy Self-Respect* in your **Personal Wisdom Wheel**
- receiving practical invitations to explore *Healthy Self-Respect* more deeply on your own and/or with others.

COURAGEOUS SELF-TRUST

In the fourth Module, we'll be:
- exploring the Council Seat of *Courageous Self-Trust*
- getting to know the *Wisdom Keeper* who's come to support us on a Collective level
- calling in the specific *Wisdom Keeper* who's meant to sit in the seat of *Courageous Self-Trust* in your **Personal Wisdom Wheel**
- receiving practical invitations to explore *Courageous Self-Trust* more deeply on your own and/or with others.

REVERENT SURRENDER

In the fifth Module, we'll be:
- exploring the Council Seat of *Reverent Surrender*
- getting to know the *Wisdom Keeper* who's come to support us on a Collective level
- calling in the specific *Wisdom Keeper* who's meant to sit in the seat of *Reverent Surrender* in your **Personal Wisdom Wheel**
- receiving practical invitations to explore *Reverent Surrender* more deeply on your own and/or with others.

CONCLUSION

Finally, in our sixth and final Module, we'll be:
- bringing our time together to a close
- reviewing the ground we've covered
- enjoying some final reflections on our time together
- receiving some resources and possibilities for further explorations, should you feel inspired to continue your journey.

I'M SO HAPPY TO BE TAKING A WALK
AROUND THE *WISDOM WHEEL* WITH YOU!

AS YOU UNCOVER THE ALCHEMY
AND WISDOM OF YOUR OWN *INTEGRITY* DANCE,
YOU WILL BE STRETCHED AND SUPPORTED.

PLEASE TAKE YOUR TIME
WITH EACH MODULE.

WHEN IT COMES TO *INTEGRITY*,
DEEP-AND-SLOW WINS THE RACE!

LET'S BEGIN WITH OUR INITIATION!

WISDOM KEEPING WORDS

Mireya Alejo Marcet, M.A., MFT
Artist, Breathworker, Sacred Altar Creatrix

"We are living in a time that is demanding all of us to 're-member' and bring forward our most unique, creative and authentic offering to ourselves, our communities and the planet as a whole.

This is the time for each of us to find our unique 'song' or 'inner essence'—the truest expression of who we are and who we wish to be in this life."

MODULE ONE

INITIATION

"In shamanism, there is a rite of passage called the quest for vision. You spend a few days alone in the forest, without water, without food, without protection. When you cross this portal, you get a new vision of the world, because you have faced your fears, your difficulties ... What world do you want to build for you? For now, this is what you can do: serenity in the storm. Calm down, pray every day. Establish a routine to meet the sacred every day. Good things emanate; what you emanate now is the most important thing. And sing, dance, resist through art, joy, faith and love."

~ White Eagle, an indigenous Hopi Wisdom Keeper

INTRODUCING YOU TO YOUR OWN DECK

The creative process behind the birth of the *Wisdom Keepers* was mysterious, whimsical and deeply intuitive. It took place during a particularly stressful time in my life, and a chaotic time in the world. I felt called to drop in, fret less and play more. I welcomed one face after another as they trickled in through my dreams and imagination.

Over time, these *64 Faces of Awakening* evolved into beings who have become friends, guides, mentors and transmitters of presence and compassion for people around the globe. I am now convinced that the *Wisdom Keepers* have come to invite all of us to embrace the whole of ourselves, relax deeply in our own skin and open our hearts to the world—even during challenging times.

The *Wisdom Keepers* represent both ancient and new human archetypes. They connect us with our collective evolution and indigenous roots. Many are elders—reminding us to honor and celebrate the tremendous wisdom carried by those who've walked the path before us.

The *Oracle Deck* is deeply inspired by Carl Jung's work with universal archetypes and the *Shadow*, as well as the I Ching, Human Design, and especially, *The Gene Keys*, brought to the world by the teacher, mystic, award-winning poet and my dear friend, Richard Rudd.

As the creator of *The Wisdom Keepers Oracle Deck & Inner Guidebook*, *The 64 Faces of Awakening Coloring Book* and many *Wisdom Keeper*-inspired projects, it is my great honor to introduce you to your very own deck. I'd like to begin by sharing what you'll find in each of the cards.

EACH CARD HAS...

A NUMBER: Each *Wisdom Keeper* is associated with one of 64 archetypes, which can be related to the 64 hexagrams of the I Ching and some of its descendants, including *The Gene Keys*. My heart's greatest intention in weaving together the *Wisdom Keepers* and *The Gene Keys* through this *Oracle Deck* is to explore how the *Wisdom Keepers* can serve people in a practical, playful, psychologically insightful and personally transformative way.

THREE WORDS: Each *Wisdom Keeper* is connected to three essential concepts, the *Shadow*, *Gift* and *Siddhi*, as used by Richard Rudd in *The Gene Keys*. These define the *Spectrum of Consciousness* and refer to archetypal states that he correlates with the human experiential stages of *Survival*, *Service* and *Surrender*. The *Shadow* has its roots in Jungian psychology. The word *Siddhi* is a Sanskrit term used in both Buddhist and Hindu mystical traditions.

A SHADOW: When we are worried about our survival and fear is in the driver's seat, we find ourselves in *Shadow* territory. Our *Shadows* can be expressed in repressive or reactive ways. They are also the gold out of which arise our liberation.

A GIFT: When we are more oriented towards serving others and honoring ourselves than protecting and defending ourselves, we more naturally share our *Gifts* and feel a sense of belonging in the world.

A SIDDHI: When we have entered a pure state of expansion and completely surrendered our sense of separateness into the Whole, we have entered the realm of the *Siddhi*.

Understanding how the *Gift*, *Shadow* and *Siddhi* are constantly interacting with each other throughout our lives can help us engage with the *Wisdom Keepers*—and ourselves—with greater compassion and patience.

FACE SYMBOLS: Each *Wisdom Keeper* has been intentionally infused with universal yet specific symbols, reflecting the unique *Gifts* embodied by them. (A **Glossary of Symbols** will be added to a Second Edition of the *Wisdom Keepers Inner Guidebook*—paperback and e-book versions. So, keep an eye out!)

A BIT MORE ABOUT THE HUMAN FACE: The human face is often called the 'organ of emotion,' one of our most powerful channels of nonverbal communication. From the moment we are born, we are constantly monitoring, mirroring and reading the faces around us, so that we can better understand what others are feeling and assess whether we are loved and safe in the world. We have the potential to heal old wounds through the formation of new loving attachments as we gaze into the *Wisdom Keepers'* faces. Just looking into a face that reflects love and acceptance can have a lasting impact on how we see and experience ourselves, as well as on our ability to give and receive love.

A WISDOM STORY: Each *Wisdom Keeper* has an archetypal yet deeply personal story.

A GIFT FOR YOU: Each *Wisdom Keeper* brings a gift of wisdom and guidance through their stories. Each story is specific to its *Wisdom Keeper*, and also has universal relevance.

A MIRROR CARD: The last card in the deck is a mirror card, reflecting your beautiful self. It can be used in a myriad of ways.

TIME TO OPEN YOUR DECK

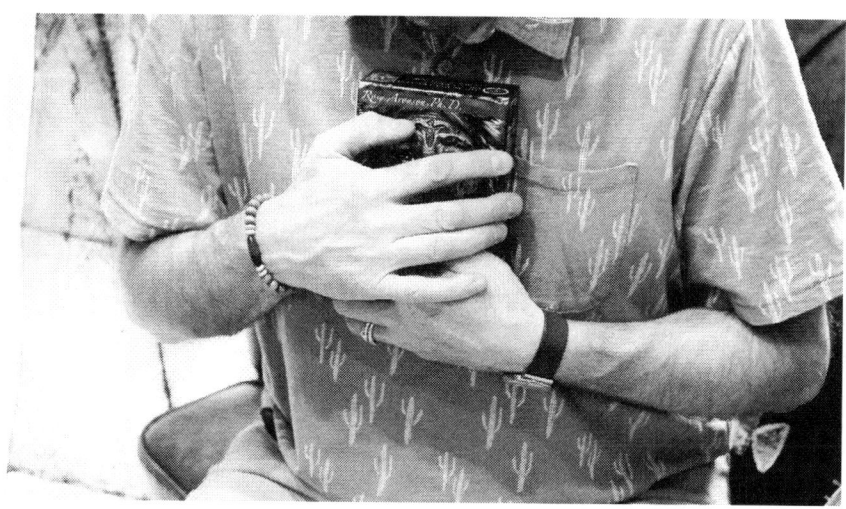

Hold your deck close to your heart, lay your hands upon it and/or envision your deck surrounded by a soft ball of energy or Chi. Bless your deck in the way that feels most right to you.

Now imagine that you're about to meet your soul family from all over the world. Sixty-four amazing beings have traveled through time and space … just to love and support you.

As you open your deck, feel your heart opening with it. Know that this is just the beginning of a deep, compassionate, healing and empowering adventure.

EXPLORING YOUR INNER GUIDEBOOK

The mini-Wisdom Keepers Inner Guidebook comes with the deck.
A larger paperback, as well as ebook version of the Guidebook, are available at www.wisdomkeepers.net.

Once you've opened your *Inner Guidebook*, give yourself some time to browse through it. You'll find lots of rich material in there. You'll learn how this deck can be used in powerful synergy with *The Gene Keys* and Human Design.

You'll find an exploration of the *Shadow*, quotes from Richard Rudd (author of *The Gene Keys*), questions to support you in your contemplation process, and practical suggestions for how to work with the cards. You'll also find lots of wonderful card spreads, and much more.

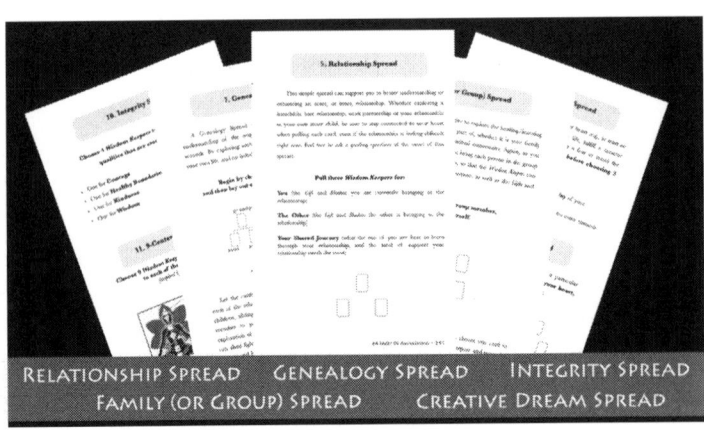

RELATIONSHIP SPREAD   GENEALOGY SPREAD   INTEGRITY SPREAD
FAMILY (OR GROUP) SPREAD   CREATIVE DREAM SPREAD

GETTING TO KNOW YOUR *WISDOM KEEPERS*

The power of this course depends greatly on your energetic connection with the *Wisdom Keepers*. I want the *Wisdom Keepers* to feel like cherished members of your soul family. So, before you get started, be sure to take a little time to get to know the *Wisdom Keepers*—up close and personal.

Begin by holding the cards in your hand, and going through them, one by one. Get a feel for each *Wisdom Keeper*. Notice how each *Wisdom Keeper* makes you feel. You might find that one speaks to you today, and others speak to you on other days. That's totally OK.

The last card in your deck is different from all of the others. It's a mirror card. (Because you, ultimately, are the *Wisdom Keeper* that you've been looking for!)

FACE DOWN

If you'd like an element of surprise when picking a card, or to allow synchronicity to connect you with your *Wisdom Keeper*, feel free to spread the cards face down. Slowly run your hand over the cards, or allow your eyes to soften while gazing at the back of the cards. Sense the energy and go from there.

FACE UP

You are equally welcome to pick your *Wisdom Keepers* with eyes open, using your intuition. There will be magic either way.

SPEND TIME WITH YOUR *WISDOM KEEPER* BEFORE TURNING TO THE BOOK

Whenever working with the *Wisdom Keepers Oracle Deck*, whether it's during this course or in your everyday practice, I encourage you to take time to simply be with your *Wisdom Keeper* before referring to the *Inner Guidebook*. Look into their eyes. Take in all of the symbols on their faces, trusting the significance will come to you at the perfect time. Allow a genuine connection to unfold between you and this being, welcoming the feelings, thoughts and associations that might arise.

OPEN YOUR INNER GUIDEBOOK

Then, in your own time, go to the page in the *Inner Guidebook* where this *Wisdom Keeper* appears. Read what you're drawn to reading.

Keep in mind that there may be parts of the *Wisdom Keeper's* story that you relate to, and parts that you don't. That's OK. You are not this *Wisdom Keeper*, but you are a *Wisdom Keeper*, with your own story and your own way of relating to the themes that are illuminated through this person's life.

In addition to using them in the **Wisdom Wheel of Integrity Course**, I encourage you to share the *Wisdom Keepers* with your friends, families and communities.

I wish you a magical, rich and ever-deepening relationship with these precious beings. May they help you to uncover the unique wisdom you are meant to bring to this powerfully transformative time in human history.

To learn more about the story behind the *Wisdom Keepers*, check out this video at:

TINYURL.COM/WISDOM-KEEPERS-STORY

PREPARING YOUR WISDOM WHEEL

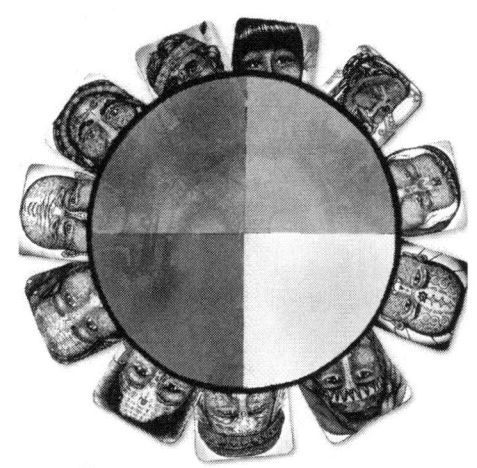

A FEW WORDS ABOUT TRADITIONAL (AND NON-TRADITIONAL) *WISDOM KEEPERS*

For centuries, Native American and indigenous cultures have identified the elders and teachers in their communities as *Wisdom Keepers. Wisdom Keepers* have been revered and trusted not only for their sharp minds, but their compassionate hearts and strong spirits. Able to embody and impart sacred, holistic teachings, and to nurture a humble-yet-potent relationship with the Great Mystery, *Wisdom Keepers* have helped their communities through hard times for generations. Both spiritually and practically, they've served their communities by bringing everyone in the tribe closer together, as well as closer to the earth and the cosmos.

Many people in today's world are like me. They're *Wisdom Seekers* who long for the healing and empowering guidance that *Wisdom Keepers* have traditionally provided in the past. But many of us have lost touch with the ways of our ancestors.

Very few of us still live in indigenous or traditional communities where elders are respected and responsible for passing down ancient, experientially-tested wisdom to the younger generations. Many of us turn to modern-day professional *Wisdom Keepers* for support and inspiration when we need it. Others of us feel like we have nowhere to turn.

This is one of the main reasons why I created the *Wisdom Keepers Oracle Deck*. I wanted to offer a loving family of *Wisdom Keepers* to people like me … and you.

Now that you've had the chance to thoroughly acquaint yourself with your own deck, you've probably noticed that many of the faces are of indigenous elders, the kinds we typically associate with traditional *Wisdom Keepers*. You've probably also noticed that some of the *Wisdom Keepers* look a bit different than the ones we often think of.

That's because these days, *Wisdom Keepers* come in all ages, shapes and sizes. Some of them look a lot like you and me. Or like the compassionate people we've known, worked with, learned from … or played with throughout our lives! There are even young *Wisdom Keepers* in this deck, because Lord knows, there are some incredibly wise children out there. And just because we're getting older doesn't necessarily mean we're getting any wiser! Wisdom is not a given.

Disclaimer:

Please know that I do not claim to be a Buddhist, a Shaman, or a traditional *Wisdom Keeper*. I like to think of myself more like a synthesis-loving *Wisdom Keeper*-in-training who is drawn to wisdom wherever I find it.

This means that this *Oracle Deck* is not an ancestral indigenous tool, although it may reflect aspects of wisdom that I've gathered over the years of personal and spiritual explorations which have been greatly inspired by earth-based, indigenous wisdom. It is not meant to be a substitute for a deep Buddhist practice, or the kind of shamanic journey that can only be taken (over a long period of time) with the guidance of someone (and ideally in the context of a community) that has been deeply steeped in the medicinal arts for generations.

A FEW WORDS ABOUT THE WHEEL

Since we will be working with a Wheel during this course (in this case a ***Wisdom Wheel of Integrity***), I'd like to take a moment to honor the Wheel as a sacred and universal symbol, one that has been utilized all over the world. I believe it holds special relevance to—and is especially suited for—an exploration of *Integrity*.

The Wheel, for example, is one of the oldest symbols in Buddhism—meaning *Perfection*. While there are many variations of the Wheel of Dharma, they usually contain eight spokes, representing the Eightfold Path (Right View, Right Intention, Right Speech, Right Action, Right Livelihood, Right Effort, Right Mindfulness and Right Meditation).

Dharma Wheels with four spokes symbolize the Four Noble Truths. (The Truth of Suffering, the Truth of the Cause of Suffering, the Truth of the End of Suffering, and the Truth of the Path that Leads to the End of Suffering).

Dharma Wheels with 24 spokes, known as the Ashoka Chakra, illuminate the 24 ideal qualities of a follower of Buddhism.

All together, the three aspects of the Dharma Wheel symbolize concentration, ethics and wisdom—all essential teachings of Buddhism. And the hub at the very center of the Dharma Wheel represents moral discipline. The reason these teachings were described as a Wheel was because they were able to move and travel throughout the land, and help relieve people of suffering by learning how to harness the mind.

In Hindu traditions, the Dharma Wheel—often found in depictions of Vishnu, is associated with law, preservation and with restoring and maintaining order in the world.

In Tibet, the Dharma Wheel is considered an Auspicious Symbol, typically placed between two deer (reminiscent of Buddha's first teachings in a deer park). This wheel reminds us that Buddha not only valued humans, but all beings … and all life. It has also been portrayed as a weapon used to overcome ignorance.

The Medicine Wheel, Sacred Hoop or Wheel of Life is also a powerful symbol used in Native American traditions and by indigenous peoples in the Americas. This symbol lives and breathes at the heart of the Shamanic path, and it will be holding and inspiring us throughout our journey.

Although there are many cultural variations of the Wheel depending on the tribe, the Medicine Wheel remains an archetypal symbol of transformation, and is most often represented by four directions—each with its corresponding season, color, element, animals and archetypal essences. In addition to the four directions, the traditional Medicine Wheel acknowledges three more Directions: Above (Father Sky), Below (Mother Earth) and Center (right where the 'sacred fire of self' sits). In this course, we will be including the Center of the Wheel along with the four directions.

The fact that the Wheel is a circle helps us to remember the cycle of life. When it comes to our lives, there is no beginning or end, no straight path we must follow to make sure we get from point A to point B, and no true division between you and me, or between me and a mountain!

One of the most essential wisdom teachings of indigenous cultures—whether Buddhist, Hindu or Native American, is that all things on earth are living. And no matter how things seem on the surface—or around the extended family dinner table (especially these days!), all beings are profoundly interconnected.

Not exactly a Wheel, but in Western mythology, we have King Arthur's round table. The round table can be seen as a symbol of shared power and *Equality*, as opposed to hierarchy and dominance. In a way, what we will be doing together in this course is inviting a council of *Wisdom Keepers* to sit down at the round table in our hearts. Each *Wisdom Keeper* is essential. Each one has a perspective that is needed. Each one gets to have a say.

Ultimately, the Wheel or Table has the potential to show us a way to live in harmony with ourselves, with our community, with nature and with Spirit. It also invites us to see all things as living—including the cards in this deck! In this way, the Wheel makes the perfect symbol for us to be using as we dive deeply into an exploration of *Integrity*.

BLACK ELK SPEAKS...

You have noticed that everything an Indian does in a circle,
and that is because the Power of the World always works in circles,
and everything tries to be round.

In the old days all our power came to us from the sacred hoop of the nation
and so long as the hoop was unbroken the people flourished.
The flowering tree was the living center of the hoop,
and the circle of the four quarters nourished it.

The East gave peace and light, the South gave warmth,
the West gave rain and the North with its cold and mighty wind gave strength and endurance.

This knowledge came to us from the outer world with our religion.

Everything the power of the world does is done in a circle.
The sky is round and I have heard that the earth is round like a ball
and so are all the stars. The wind, in its greatest power, whirls.
Birds make their nests in circles, for theirs is the same religion as ours.
The sun comes forth and goes down again in a circle. The moon
does the same and both are round. Even the seasons form a great
circle in their changing and always come back again to where they were.

The life of a man is a circle from childhood to childhood, and so it is
in everything where power moves. Our teepees were round like the
nests of birds, and these were always set in a circle, the nation's hoop,
a nest of many nests, where the Great Spirit meant for us to hatch our children.

~ Black Elk, Holy Man of the Oglala Sioux 1863-1950

GETTING YOUR OWN WISDOM WHEEL READY

Before we pick our first card together, (the *Wisdom Keeper* that will sit at the very center of our **Wisdom Wheel**, the one who will lovingly witness and bring balance to our process of *Integrity* building), let's prepare the ground.

Take out a large sheet of paper and place it somewhere that feels like a good place to have your spread.

Take a marker or pencil, and draw a simple Medicine Wheel—a large circle with four quadrants.

Be sure to make your circle big enough so that there's room to place four cards, each at a quarter point along the circle, and one in the center of the circle.

We will be pulling cards all together over the course of our *Integrity* Journey. I will be pulling cards on behalf of the Collective, to shed light on our shared journey together.

And each of you will be pulling your own cards to reflect your unique journey.

As I mentioned before, I encourage you to find a calm, sacred place for your **Wisdom Wheel**—ideally somewhere where the Wheel can remain over the coming days and weeks. I'd like you to be able to visit your **Wisdom Wheel** whenever you like, and to feel like you have a place where your *Wisdom Keeper* Council lives and is available to provide you with love, insight and guidance.

WHO SITS AT THE HEART OF YOUR PERSONAL WHEEL

Now that you've prepared your **Wisdom Wheel**, it's time to begin the journey. I invite you to call in the *Wisdom Keeper* who is meant to sit at the very center of your **Wheel of Integrity**, right where the sacred fire of your 'self' lives.

Sit in front of your **Wisdom Wheel**. Make sure you've got a journal and pen right there, in case you want to use it. Now spread all of your cards out, face up.

We are working with the 'self' here, so let's keep our eyes open. Bring a soft awareness to this process, as you gently gaze upon the faces in front of you. Notice which of the *Wisdom Keeper* faces call you. Pick the card that—for whatever reason—pulls you closest, or just feels right. Place it in front of you. Whether or not your rational mind understands your choice, I ask that you trust your choice. This is an important *Wisdom Keeper* for you, and it has great relevance for the themes you'll be exploring.

Now take some time to simply look into the eyes of the *Wisdom Keeper* you've chosen if the eyes are open, or just take in the face. Pay attention to your breathing as you do so. Notice if it quickens, softens, relaxes, or something else. Notice other subtle sensations in your body, if there are any. Notice how this *Wisdom Keeper* makes you feel. See if you can establish a heart connection with your *Wisdom Keeper*. You might even want to lift the card and rest it on your heart for a few breaths, receiving the love this being has come to offer you.

If you're tempted to pick up the book, see if you can wait. Spend just a little more time taking in the symbols in the face. Notice the number on the card. Notice the word on the card. Allow your imagination to engage with these aspects of the *Wisdom Keeper*. Do any memories arise? Any simple insights? Do you have any mental associations with the word or number of the card?

Jot down any thoughts, feelings or insights that have come up for you in your journal. If you have no words, feel free to doodle a symbol, or put down some color on the page that reflects how you're feeling. Any and all expressions are welcome.

Now, I'd like to invite you to place your *Wisdom Keeper* in the heart of your **Wisdom Wheel** and communicate with your *Wisdom Keeper* directly.

In your own words, (whether written in your journal, spoken out loud or inside of you), ask your Center's *Wisdom Keeper* for guidance and support. Let them know that you are wanting to deepen your understanding of *Integrity*, that you want to know what it means for YOU to live your life with *Integrity*. Let them know that you're going to be spending time exploring this theme in the coming days and weeks, that you're going to need their help, and that you're open to their guidance. Make sure your *Wisdom Keeper* knows that even if at first, you can't see the connection or relevance of what they're offering, you are committed to remaining open to discovering what their gift for you might be over time. Add anything else that feels right to you.

PRACTICAL INVITATIONS TO EXPLORE MORE DEEPLY

QUESTIONS TO EXPLORE

Here are some simple questions for you to explore on your own, to help you connect even more deeply with this *Wisdom Keeper* who has been called to sit at the very center of your **Wisdom Wheel of Integrity**. Feel free to write your responses down in your journal. If other questions arise for you, answer them too—or instead. Trust yourself. These are just prompts to get you started.

- What does this particular *Wisdom Keeper* inspire in you?

- What important truth does he or she remind you of?

- Which of your Gifts does this *Wisdom Keeper* see and trust?

- Which of your Shadows might this being understand and embrace?

- If this *Wisdom Keeper* had a message for you today about *Integrity*, what would it be?

- If you were to sit down and have a conversation with this person about something you're really struggling with these days, what would you want to share or ask?

- How do you imagine your *Wisdom Keeper* would respond?

DIVE INTO THE BOOK

Now it's time to take out your book and find the page that corresponds with your *Wisdom Keeper* at the **Center of the Wheel**. **At your own pace, do the following:**

1. Read Richard Rudd's quote.

2. Look at the *Gene Keys*-inspired Shadow, Siddhi and Gift words connected to this *Wisdom Keeper*.

3. Allow your mind to add the word *Integrity* to the mix, without thinking too hard. Just let it be there … like a planted seed. If you can't see a connection yet, no worries.

4. Read the story of your *Wisdom Keeper*.

5. Now read the Gift for You Section.

6. Remember that the *Wisdom Keepers* are unique individuals, with their own life experience. Your *Wisdom Keeper* has come to understand the nature of the Gift, Shadow and Siddhi (or spiritual essence) that they carry, in their own way. You don't have to relate to the story of your *Wisdom Keeper* right now. You may relate to certain aspects of it and not others. This is just one story of how one being came to experience a shadow, embody a gift and connect with a spiritual essence. Your story is yours, equally rich, equally fascinating, equally full of potential.

7. What you learn about this *Wisdom Keeper* through the book doesn't have to contradict or cancel out what you received on your own—intuitively, without words. It can all co-exist. One of the most important qualities of all Keepers of Wisdom is the ability to hold paradox.

8. Another universal *Wisdom Keeper* quality is *Patience*. It will likely take time for all of the *Integrity* pieces to fall into place. So, you may instantly feel a connection between this *Wisdom Keeper* and the theme of *Integrity*, or you may have no clue. Perhaps the best you can do right now is receive a simple bit of inspiration. Perhaps a phrase touches you. Or you just get a feeling. Or there's something about a look in the eye that awakens something in you, and you don't know what it is. That's all OK.

9. Look through the Questions for Contemplation. Perhaps one or two will open up a door for you. See whether any of the questions in particular connect you to the theme of *Integrity*.

10. Jot any insights, questions or doodles down in your journal.

11. If you are familiar with *The Gene Keys*, this particular *Wisdom Keeper* may correspond with a Gene Key that you have in your profile. Allow what you know about this Gene Key and its unique placement in your profile to creatively synergize with the theme of *Integrity*. See what happens!

SHARE WITH OTHERS

I invite you to share your experience with this *Wisdom Keeper* with a friend, or inside of a small group of trusted people. Let your fellow explorer(s) know which *Wisdom Keeper* called you and is now sitting at the heart of your **Wisdom Wheel of Integrity**. Take turns sharing whichever aspect of your journey you've found most inspiring, challenging or interesting. Share from your journal or simply from your heart. Make sure that you create a safe space where you and others know that whatever you share will be held confidential, as well as respected. You might want to come up with basic sharing and listening guidelines to be sure that everyone feels safe.

Simple Guidelines for Sharing:

- Remember that you don't have to share anything that you don't feel comfortable sharing.
- Trust your intuition to tell you what to share, when to share it, how much to share and with whom.
- Remember that all experiences can offer us sacred-symbolic food for the soul. If you have the impulse to share an experience, trust your impulse. There's likely a gift in there for you.
- While you're sharing, allow yourself time to be silent, to pause and to feel.
- Remember not only to share the content, but your felt experience. You may actually **only** want to share your felt experience, and to keep the content to yourself. That's perfectly OK.

Guidelines for Listening:

- Be present. Open your heart. Relax your mind.
- Welcome silence and feelings.
- Notice and breathe through any impulses you may feel to provide an interpretation or help your partner find answers.
- Hold what is being shared with you as though it is sacred.
- Honor confidentiality.
- If you would like to ask your partner a deepening question or provide feedback, ask your partner if they feel open to a response from you. If they'd prefer you simply listen, receive their request graciously and trust that your presence is more than enough.
- If your partner or a group member has shared something that has touched you personally or enriched your self-understanding, express your gratitude.

WHO SITS AT THE HEART
OF OUR COLLECTIVE WHEEL

"If you allow your pain, or the world pain, to be expressed through an artistic process, you will see alchemy in progress."

~ Richard Rudd

Gift: *Imagination*
Shadow: *Confusion*
Siddhi: *Illumination*

I'd like to end our INITIATION MODULE by sharing the *Wisdom Keeper* that I drew for all of us. This is the *Wisdom Keeper* who will be sitting at the very heart of our **Collective Wisdom Wheel of Integrity** over the coming days and weeks.

The card I pulled (with closed eyes, since I wasn't pulling it just for myself but on behalf of all of us) is the *Wisdom Keeper* of *Imagination*.

If this is the same *Wisdom Keeper* you've pulled, this likely means that—at the very heart of your experience of *Integrity*—the personal and collective are interwoven. They are probably also amplifying each other. I encourage you to already begin to notice how the *Integrity* themes (or lack of *Integrity* themes!) you're noticing in the outer world might be mirroring something happening within you, or in your personal life.

If you drew a different *Wisdom Keeper* than the one I picked, find the *Wisdom Keeper* of *Imagination* in your deck, and place her in the middle of your **Wheel of Integrity**, right next to your *Wisdom Keeper*. So basically, you should have a pair of *Wisdom Keepers* right in the middle of your Wheel, holding the center together. As I share about the *Wisdom Keeper* of *Imagination*, I invite you to let your own imagination help you uncover possible areas of thematic synergy between the two.

Personally, I was so happy when I pulled this card. I think it's such a good one for all of us. Lord knows, if there's a shadow state that's running rampant around the planet at the moment, it's the shadow of Confusion.

OK, now I'm going to share from the *Wisdom Keepers* Inner Guidebook. Feel free to sit back and relax in a cozy chair with a cup of tea as you read.

MY WISDOM STORY

My grandparents suffered unspeakable cruelty during the war. They managed to escape with my parents just before the rest of their family was brutally killed. They never spoke of what happened, and my parents knew not to ask. Instead of looking back, my parents devoted their lives to providing their children a safe and secure future, free of persecution, by focusing on our successful assimilation and keeping our family's pain snugly under the rug.

As a young girl, I wanted to please them, so I did my best to imitate those around me and kept my questions about our family's past to myself. But I felt out of place, like something essential was 'off.' To the outside world, my family seemed perfect. But at home, it felt like living with a herd of elephants in the room. I often felt confused and uneasy, figuring I was just too sensitive, intense and weird.

When the pain of not knowing where we came from got too great, I became determined to solve the mystery. I secretly studied all there was to know about the country my grandparents came from and my family's own tragic history in the war. Finally, it made sense—the sheep-like behavior, the stubborn evasiveness about the past. At first my revelations lessened my confusion and increased my compassion towards my parents. But when they still refused to talk about any of it, I became angry with them for refusing to deal with their pain or talk about anything that actually mattered. I was tired of being repressed by their repression.

One day, when I couldn't take it anymore, I cruelly accused my parents of cowardice, and then I flaunted graphic pictures from their past in front of them. Suddenly, in the midst of my outburst, my father clutched his chest in pain. Though he survived the heart attack, I was devastated and unable to forgive myself. Racked with guilt, I found a counselor who specialized in healing the wounds of history. With his support, I learned how, through my relentless attempts to end the confusion, I was avoiding my own pain, just like my family. So, I let my mind go blank and my heart feel the pure suffering of my people.

That's when the miracles started, and my *Imagination* was unleashed. Now my life is a work of art, and everything I do is infused with the kind of light that can only emerge through darkness.

MY GIFT TO YOU

I come to set your *Imagination* free. But first, you must bless your pain and confusion with the gift of your awareness. In the presence of confusion, there is nothing to do. Nowhere to go. Nothing to figure out. Confusion is a totally natural human state. It is actually holy ground. So, taste it. Embrace it. But do not try to change, interpret or get rid of it. As soon as you remember that you are not your confusion, its true diamond nature will emerge from the coal. And your *Imagination* will be released, so that you can give expression to your pain and inner demons through a fulfilling process of creativity. Whether you're expressing with a paintbrush or a pen, be honest, courageous, illogical and wild. Go where no one else has gone before.

PRACTICAL INVITATIONS TO EXPLORE MORE DEEPLY

Feel free to write your responses down in your journal. If other questions arise for you, answer them too—or instead. Trust yourself. These are just prompts to get you started.

QUESTIONS FOR CONTEMPLATION

What are the ways you avoid feeling pain and confusion?

By fitting in? Overthinking? Keeping busy? Multi-tasking? Screen-binging? Protesting? Star-gazing? Affirmation-writing? Getting angry? Too much care-taking?

In relation to what is happening in our world, are you throwing yourself into frenetic activism, judging people harshly who see things differently than you?

Are you avoiding everything by clinging to affirmations or New Age clichés, pretending that everything is OK when deep down, you don't feel this is true?

Are you feeling depressed, overwhelmed and paralyzed?

Where are you still hiding your originality?

How do your current relationships reinforce your hiding?

How might this hiding be impacting your *Integrity*? What are you afraid might happen if you came out of hiding? Even if you felt more in your *Integrity*, might others see you in a lesser light?

Can you think of someone who made a difference in the world through their art, their music, their writing, their creative approach to business, their *Imagination*?

Think of someone whose *Integrity* is enriched by their *Imagination*. Allow the thought of them to inspire you.

At this moment, think about the world you're living in, the way you're showing up in your full *Integrity*, or not showing up. What causes you the most pain or confusion?

Find a simple creative way to express your pain, fear or confusion. Don't make it great art. Make it honest. And then find a way to 'lovingly hold' this expression. For example, you could create a little nest for it with a scarf, and place it inside. You could place it lovingly inside of a beautiful box that has sacred meaning to you. The point is to create a safe space for your pain and confusion to rest … without being judged, prodded or pushed away.

Just for this moment, let yourself be like Martin Luther King Jr. Set your *Imagination* free to dream up the world you want us all to live in.

Fill in the blank. "I have a dream! My dream is…"

taken like a scarf i live freely, No + Everything moves effortlessly I envision myself engaging with people of all cultures feeling so at peace i'm with my soulmate, i'm in love with myself. I'm Confident, i'm playful i'm so Excited + grateful for each + Everyday. i am well known + inspiring My life is exciting from within, i love Sex. i love Myself, My Expression is freeflowing. i bring Joy wherever i Go but also Show People theres a place for Everyone + Embrace everysingle Emotion of Mine

MODULE TWO

"My religion is simple. My religion is kindness."

~ The Dalai Lama

WISDOM KEEPING WORDS

Sharon Kukunda
Teacher & Executive Director of Universal Love Alliance of Uganda

"For me, Loving-Kindness means embodying tenderness and showing consideration towards others. My life experience has taught me how to be kind, tolerant, and to treat my fellow human beings with love, respect and care—no matter the situation, no matter how others are perceiving or treating me, or whether or not I will be rewarded. The ups and downs in my life have taught me to trust that even the most difficult and painful experiences have the potential to play out and unfold positively over time.

Nothing gives me greater joy or matters more to me than the love of diversity. I am committed to non-violence and am often looking for opportunities to work for justice. I have learned to say 'yes' to all of who I am, even the parts of me that are not perfect or different from others. This has helped me become someone who is able to be loving, kind, considerate, inclusive and respectful of others."

WHAT IS *LOVING-KINDNESS?*
AND WHY IS IT NECESSARY TO *INTEGRITY?*

Often when we think about being in our *Integrity*, we think about speaking our truth and living in accordance with our highest principles. We think *Integrity* requires that we know what's right, and we do what's right. There can, of course, be truth in this—especially when our truth is based on principles of fairness, *Equality* and compassion.

But sometimes, in our attempts to be honest, to speak our truth, and to do the right thing, we forget to be kind. We forget that most people come to be who they are honestly. We forget that much of the time—behind the behavior and attitudes we find so difficult to understand and deal with in other people—is a good amount of suffering, ignorance or fear.

For those of us who've spent a good chunk of our lives trying to understand the human species and the world around us, it can be especially hard to admit that we don't have a corner on Truth.

No matter how much our own perceptions, principles and values make sense to us, they also reflect the sum total of our life experience—the blessings that stem from our privilege, and the limitations that come from our conditioning.

Just like the people who act in ways that drive us crazy and are so hard for us to understand, we also carry our unique brand of wounding. We live at the mercy of our own fears, whether they are conscious or unconscious. And no matter how much we've learned, or think we know, no matter how subtle, seemingly small or unintentional our unkind transgressions might be, we can be just as guilty of acting out of our own ignorance.

If you are drawn to this course, I wouldn't be surprised if sometimes you forget to be kind to yourself. Many people who have the deep desire to make a positive difference in the world live with the burden of standards that are way too high. We live with this constant nagging feeling that we're not doing enough, that we're not doing it right, that we're failing to live up to our ideals. Our attempts to be and act from a place of *Integrity* can lead to self-criticism.

Remember how in the beginning of this course I spoke of the dictionary definitions of *Integrity*. One part of the definition had to do with living in accordance with a moral code. The other part had to do with achieving a state of wholeness—of integrating, embracing all of our parts. Even those parts that aren't anywhere near perfect.

So, what does this mean? It means that when it comes to *Loving-Kindness*, when it comes to becoming WHOLE in relation to this aspect of *Integrity*, we need to practice kindness towards ourselves too!

It also means that we have to stay awake to the inner critic. Because very few of us can be kind to everyone all of the time. Even fewer of us can be kind to ourselves all of the time! Especially these days, when many of us are living in a completely emotionally overwhelming world, when every time we turn on the TV, or check our smart phones, or walk out the door, it's like walking right up to a fear buffet!

This is why when I think of *Loving-Kindness*, I think of a resilient heart. Not a heart that's always open, but a heart that has thoroughly practiced the art of opening back up—after understandable (and frequent) moments of constriction.

So, it is in the spirit of a Resilient Heart that I now call upon the *Wisdom Keeper* who will sit in the Collective seat of *Loving-Kindness*.

Let's see who comes to us!

"We can never obtain peace in the outer world until we make peace with ourselves."

~ the Dalai Lama

WHO SITS IN THE COLLECTIVE SEAT OF
LOVING-KINDNESS?

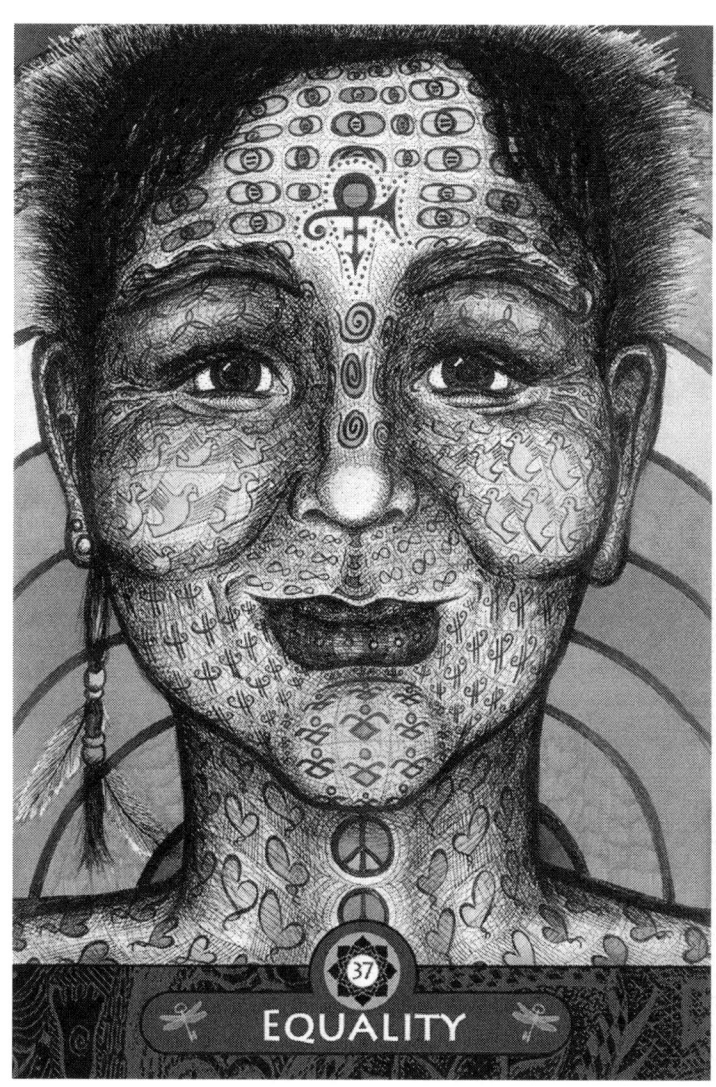

*"From the point of view of the human heart,
all humanity is one family."*

~ Richard Rudd

Gift: *Equality*
Shadow: *Weakness*
Siddhi: *Tenderness*

The *Wisdom Keeper* I pulled on behalf of the collective, the *Wisdom Keeper* who shall be sitting in the seat of *Loving-Kindness* over the coming days and weeks, is the *Wisdom Keeper* of *Equality* and *Tenderness*. This is a profound card. And the more I feel into it, the more I feel it speaks straight to the art of cultivating a resilient heart, in the face of tremendous inner and outer resistance.

So, let me start by sharing the story of this *Wisdom Keeper* with you, and then their Gift to You. Let yourself really enjoy reading this story. Get a cup of tea and relax at your favorite reading spot. Ask your heart and soul to open up to receiving the wisdom, power and healing offered to you by this dear friend and ally.

MY WISDOM STORY

Though I was born into a girl's body, I always felt like a boy deep down. My family was conventional. My father worked; my mother took care of the children and was completely dependent on him financially. He often treated her disrespectfully and with cruelty, as if she were weak, overly sentimental and only nice to look at.

As I got older, I saw men like him ruling the world. So, I rejected my father, the patriarchy, as well as the boy in me. In absolute solidarity with my mother, I would be a girl, no matter how painful or wrong it felt within. Without realizing it, I spent the following years using every 'masculine' muscle I had to idealize and fight for all things 'feminine.' I envisioned and worked for a world where women were the leaders. I became an activist and speaker, empowering women worldwide with my ideals. I also became financially independent and bartered with 'the big boys' for rights and privileges on behalf of women everywhere.

Privately, though, I was an emotional wreck. I alienated my romantic partners constantly with unfair and cruel accusations and an insatiable need for emotional processing. The truth was that deep-down I was fighting for one thing: acceptance. But I couldn't even give that to myself. I was too weak to share, much less own, how I felt inside or how I wanted to live my life. I had zero trust that my romantic partners would still love me as a man. Nor trust that the world would ever accept a freak like me. I was convinced that if my feminist community discovered how I really felt inside, they'd no longer see me as a leader, but as an outsider, maybe even an enemy.

When the pain of hiding from myself was too great, I decided to drive to a transgender support group in a town where I'd never be recognized. I sat in the back of the room and just listened. My own story was told, over and over again, by different people. Because of their courage, I found myself: my pain, longing, loneliness … and overwhelming fear. At the end of the meeting, someone came up to me. To my shock, it was someone I knew. I expected an attack, but instead, I was given the most tender embrace. In that moment, I knew I'd find my way back to me and that I wouldn't have to do it alone.

MY GIFT TO YOU

A note before reading: See if you can feel the *Tenderness* in this *Wisdom Keeper*'s words. See if you can allow this *Tenderness* to soften your shoulders, your breath, your body, as you listen.

I am your friend. I have deep respect for you. I don't want you to change who you are at your core. You are a completely unique, worthy being, and there is a place for you in this world of ours. I see you with deep *Tenderness*. It is time to take your place, with pride, humility and profound self-acceptance. When you look at yourself, see your *Weakness* and vulnerability as your strengths. When you look out at the world, see beyond polarities, beyond gender stereotypes, beyond patriarchy and matriarchy. Aim your eye towards synthesis, to the entire continuum of beauty available to all of us. *Equality* is your birthright. You and me, we are family.

REFLECTIONS

Ahhhh … You and me. We are family.

Just take that in. We are family.

No matter how differently we look. No matter how differently we think, feel, identify or express that identity. No matter how differently we believe, act or seem. We are family. We are each essential parts of a giant whole. And, each of our inner parts make us the whole of who we are.

So, this *Wisdom Keeper* of *Equality* and *Tenderness* has come to teach all of us something about being whole and undivided—both as a human family that has come together in unity, where all members are accepted and embraced as worthy beings. And, as individual human beings, where all of our parts are welcome, where all aspects of ourselves—even those parts we find it hardest to love—are here to be listened to, understood, and ultimately embraced.

I am reminded of Rumi's Guest House. You've probably heard that poem before, but I want to share a small passage from it, so we can all breathe it in … in the context of this particular *Wisdom Keeper* who has come to teach us something important about *Loving-Kindness* and what it requires of us.

A SMALL PASSAGE FROM *THE GUEST HOUSE*

This being human is a guest house.
Every morning a new arrival.
A joy, a depression, a meanness,
some momentary awareness comes
as an unexpected visitor.
Welcome and entertain them all!
…
Be grateful for whatever comes.
because each has been sent
as a guide from beyond.

~ Jellaludin Rumi

At first when I drew this card for this course, I felt a little nervous. This *Wisdom Keeper*'s story touches on a deeply charged subject in our world today. One that has been at the heart of so much pain and fear. One that has instigated so much violence and been used to drive wedges between people in families, at work, in religious communities, in political communities, in government, in societies all over the world. Even people who would normally consider themselves to be open-minded and progressive have gotten lost in the manifestations of divisiveness that are depicted in this complex and layered story.

In a way, it feels perfect that it is a transgendered *Wisdom Keeper* who has come to help us explore the many ways in which we can be swept up in a tidal wave of collective division. It is so easy to lose touch with our potential for becoming **whole** people inside of a diverse yet **whole** humanity.

In so many of our childhood homes and early relationships, centuries of gender oppression, competition, conditioning and wounding play themselves out. Multi-generational seeds of division are planted between parents and between siblings before we've even learned to speak.

In our communities, unacknowledged and unhealed ancestral and cultural wounding spread endless forms of conflict.

And I'm not only talking about ultra-conservative or fundamentalist communities here … where one might expect strong and harsh biases against women or certain marginalized groups of people. I'm talking about the kind of division that can show up in communities where you wouldn't expect it—in progressive, spiritual communities where members pride themselves in being open-minded, compassionate and willing to stand up for the rights of marginalized peoples or important-yet-neglected causes.

Instead of looking for common ground and joining forces, too many members of oppressed groups (or advocates for important causes) end up getting lost in identity politics or clinging tightly to their particular approaches to social/spiritual change.

Instead of forming alliances and strengthening our human family and shared planet, we end up turning against each other in a competition for empathy, attention, validation and justice. We end up in a big messy fight for peace!

The way many transgendered people have been (and are still) treated around the world shows just how extreme and destructive a viscerally, culturally and politically inflamed prejudice against a group of human beings can be.

This *Wisdom Keeper*'s story also shows how an outer experience of discrimination or oppression can lead to a very painful internalized sense of self-loathing.

The transgendered movement has become one of the most politically charged subjects in recent years. There are so many perspectives on it, from one extreme to the other.

You'll find people who blame the phenomenon on too much fluoride in the water, on some secret illuminati plot to control the population or manipulate public opinion.

Some believe that the "Transgender Issue," "Political Correctness Policing" and "Cancel Culture" are being used intentionally by conservative religious and political groups in order to infiltrate, create divisions within and ultimately weaken progressive movements.

Some believe this is another example of a manufactured culture war, here to provide people with a mass distraction, so that we're all so caught up in identity politics that we won't notice what governmental policies are doing to the environment, what proxy wars are being fought in our name, and how many innocent people are being killed on behalf of the self-interest of the one percent.

Then, there are those who remind us that transgendered people have not only always been around, but they've actually been revered in indigenous cultures all over the world. Before they were pushed into the closet, they were seen and honored as spiritual teachers and medicinal healers.

Many evolutionary thinkers believe that transgenderism, gender fluidity, androgyny and the growing rainbow of human expression that seems to be emerging around the globe are signs of our shared evolution.

They believe we are all moving towards greater freedom, authenticity, wholeness and fluidity … where the human spirit can come to its fullest expression, and where individuals can allow their true authentic natures to emerge without having to carry generations and generations of heavy, constricting conditioning on their backs. People like this *Wisdom Keeper* are simply pointing us in this colorful, permission-giving direction we're all headed.

However you happen to look at Transgenderism, and wherever you fall on the gender identity/expression or orientation continuum, I'd like you to look at the ways in which you can relate to this *Wisdom Keeper*, this human being. Your story might be extremely different on the surface. But I bet underneath, you'll be able to find some parallels. This is a human story, an archetypal hero's journey kind of story, where someone is learning how to embrace themselves lovingly so that they can be themselves fully in the world and make their unique contribution.

In order for them to do that, they need to be received with *Loving-Kindness*, with *Tenderness* … by someone, somewhere. Only *Kindness*, only being seen and received as part of a loving human family, has the power to help them begin to open their heart up to themselves … and begin their true life, where they are no longer hiding in a closet, or rejecting some essential part of themselves.

That's most of us right there.

This *Wisdom Keeper* is offering you a chance to look at those parts of yourself that have been forced into and/or have found a home in the closet. Those parts that—for whatever reason—have felt forbidden, charged, controversial or just plain unsafe to acknowledge, embrace or express.

Your story is your story. Only you know what your conditioning has been throughout your life—as a young child, as a teenager, as a young adult, as a mature adult. Only you know what has been forced to live its days in the closet. It might be your sexuality; it might be your anger; it might be your irreverent humor; it might be one of your most shame-inducing insecurities; it might be a traumatic experience you've never talked about; it might be your spiritual views; it might be your political leanings; it might be the fact that you're totally into super weird paranormal research (like me).

My guess is that some of your passionate talented glorious light has also been hiding in the closet—if not now, then at some point in your past.

One thing I've found, and you might relate to this, is that things aren't so clear cut. Certain aspects of yourself may feel safe to express in one environment or community, but not in others. If you're like me, you may have a pretty big range of possible expressions.

Some people know me as a super social being. Others know me as a total introvert. A few people who know me really well know me as a total goofball. One of my cousins once described me as a very serious person who almost never speaks. I bet that's not your impression of me right now. I can hardly shut up!

This is why you'll rarely find me happily throwing big birthday parties for myself, where all of the people I know—from all walks of life—gather together in one place.

So, it makes sense that each of us has a very unique (often winding, confusing and chopped up) path towards finding and expressing our true nature.

Here's another example from my life: One of the most painful and confusing True Nature struggles I experienced was when I was in the process of making a decision about how I wanted to give birth to my daughter. My parents were very caring, responsible people who'd grown up with largely mainstream values. My father was a traditional pediatrician, and although my mother insisted on not receiving pain medication during the delivery of her two daughters (which was quite a big deal at the time), both of my parents felt extremely strongly that I should give birth in a hospital. Anything else to them was not only frightening, but a deeply irresponsible thing to do. Making a choice like that, to them at the time, was the equivalent of putting my baby and myself in harm's way. It would be almost unforgivable.

On the other hand, I had spent eight years of my life working within a highly alternative community where the ideal birth experience was supposed to take place in the ocean and end with an orgasm! Or at least it would happen at home in a hot tub and require no medication. To this spiritual/professional community, birth was supposed to be a natural process, something to be trusted and surrendered to. Sometimes hospitals were needed, but those were rare cases. Most often, hospitals were guilty of treating pregnancy like an illness and initiating a cascade of interventions that could lead to all sorts of complications that could ultimately be harmful to both mother and baby. In this environment, intentionally choosing a hospital birth and pain medication was seen as the deeply irresponsible thing to do.

It took me quite a while to cut through these two potent streams of opposing conditioning and find the approach that was right for me … the approach which would necessarily include the humbling realization that I (and most birthing mothers learn at some point!) … ultimately, had very little control over how my baby would be born. I could certainly set my intentions, and provide the best possible conditions to support those intentions. But then I'd have to let go and surrender. My daughter's birth, of course, was not the first or last time, or the only life arena, where I've had to learn that very humbling lesson!

My point in sharing this personal story is to show how we can feel pulled, prodded and shoved in so many directions—depending on where we come from, who's around us, and what we're trying to accomplish (including survive!).

It's not easy to be a multi-faceted human being trying to navigate our way through a pretty crazy world when so much is at stake. When we might be thrown out of the proverbial tribe for being or expressing who we are. Or worse.

This is probably also why I was so attracted to Human Design all of those years ago, which is essentially an authenticity practice. And why I was ultimately led to *The Gene Keys*, which if boiled down to its essence, is a *Kindness* practice. A *Kindness* practice in the face of our personal and collective shadows.

This is also why I ended up creating the *Wisdom Keepers*, with their uniquely human stories and their loving, accepting gazes. One of the most important gifts the *Wisdom Keepers* were meant to bring us doesn't involve words at all. It's simply their ability to receive us lovingly into their hearts. To give us a feeling that we are OK, just as we are. No matter what.

And then, of course, there's the 65th card, which is a mirror card … offering each of us a chance to quite literally look upon ourselves with *Loving-Kindness*.

All of this is just to say how happy I am that the *Wisdom Keeper* of *Equality* and *Tenderness* came to us, and will be an *Integrity* Council member, sitting in the collective seat of *Loving-Kindness*.

I'm going to place this *Wisdom Keeper* in this collective seat of *Loving-Kindness,* on behalf of all of us. You are welcome to do the same now if you like. Or, if you'd prefer, keep this *Wisdom Keeper* inside of your deck, in case you serendipitously choose it when it's your turn to choose a *Wisdom Keeper* for your **Personal Wheel of Integrity**, and that's fine too.

Whether you've placed this card on your **Personal Wheel** or not, let's take a look at it. When we look at this *Wisdom Keeper,* let's be reminded of how much all of us—as a collective—need each other to mirror back to us our innate lovability, our deep-down innocence, our goodness. We need to practice *Tenderness.*

Let's remember that if humanity is going to develop *Integrity* together, we're just going to have to be a little more kind. If we are to uncover what true *Equality* looks and **feels** like, we're going to need to be tender with each other.

Don't get me wrong here. We don't have to agree with everyone, relate to everyone or be passive doormats. We don't have to work with everyone, live with everyone or become friends with everyone. But we don't have to be so mean.

Let me give an example here. Over these past years, as our world has become increasingly crazy, and our mainstream news has become more of an entertainment channel than a place for investigative journalism to flourish, I've found myself looking to today's comedians for commentary on world events. A lot of the time, the laughter and relief I feel, as the comedians call out hypocrisy and acknowledge important truths with sensitivity, with insightful satire, is like a healing balm to my soul.

One thing I love about my favorite comedians is that they are not afraid of admitting to their own imperfections. It's their raw authenticity and their willingness to lay bare their utter humanity that gives them credibility in my eyes. I'm not saying that no comedians are in the business of hiding some super-sized *Weaknesse*s. But, I do believe that on the whole, the self-berating comedic profession has a better chance of producing people of '*Integrity*' than the conventional political realm, where politicians (in order to survive) are forced to project an image of absolute perfection—going back to their day of birth. In my opinion, that's a total recipe for an *Integrity* disaster.

Still, there have been times when I've also encountered my favorite truth-speaking, keenly insightful comedians—who stand on compassionate political platforms—resorting to a level of meanness that has left me feeling very uncomfortable.

When insightful and satiric commentary drops to a personal level of viciousness, when public figures—and their partners and children, and their appearance and personal inadequacies are ripped apart for all to see, when their right to exist on the planet is seriously questioned, something just doesn't feel right. And it doesn't matter how humane the comedian's political platform is, or the important point the comedian is trying to make. Something about the whole situation just feels bad. My *Integrity* antennas go 'ick.'

These comedians are, of course, only showing us what we do in our own lives. They're just doing it on a bigger scale, on the screen, in a way that allows us to laugh at other people's expense without feeling responsible. Because we're not the ones saying the words.

But what we're doing by laughing—and 'tuning in' to the show—is we're giving our consent. We're joining the Mean Team. We're participating in a subtle form of cruelty that's not good for our *Integrity* health.

And, these comedians are holding up an *Integrity* mirror for us. They're asking us to refine our taste and ability to discern between the kind of truth-telling that changes the world for the better and wakes people up … and, the kind that—even if it's hilarious—just brings us all down.

The truth is that many of us who would otherwise be funny in a gentler way, get mean when we're feeling afraid, exhausted, exacerbated, desperate and disillusioned. And there are so many reasons for all of us to be feeling that way, including today's hard-working comedians who can't even sleep or take a seven-hour vacation without missing out on some seemingly essential and crazy-making piece of news, in need of their commentary. But if we're really wanting to develop our *Integrity* muscles, it would behoove us to do a little check-in now and then. And see how we're living up to our *Loving-Kindness* ideals.

Sarah Silverman is one of my favorite comedians who I think has done a particularly good job of transcending the political and social divide that's currently spreading around the globe. While her comedy often addresses social taboos and controversial topics (like racism, sexism, politics and religion), and she's as irreverent as they come, she has gone out of her way to connect with all sorts of people, especially those whose world views are quite different than hers. She uses her humor—and her understanding that people have more in common than we think, including the love of laughter—to break down defenses and open hearts. She understands that not everyone may agree on every social issue or who should be the leader of a country. But most people know what a bad case of diarrhea feels like! And in the end, most people know what it feels like to care about someone deeply, and how good it feels to be loved.

Two things I heard her say on a podcast that I like to keep in my back packet:

"Find someone who doesn't deserve love, and give it to them."

"What?! Is compassion so expensive that we can't waste any of it on the wrong people?"

That brings me to my next point: Being honest about areas where we can improve doesn't give us the license to treat ourselves like crap. We don't have to be mean or cutting towards ourselves either.

Being willing to pick up the piercing blade of Love and Truth may be necessary these days, but we need to be sure we're not using that knife in order to cut off rejected pieces of ourselves and throw them in closets. I think the pressure to be Politically or Spiritually Correct all of the time (which is different than what I was just talking about, which has more to do with an energetic) creates horrible internal conditions for people wanting to do, think and say the right thing. The desire to think and speak perfectly can make self-honesty and inner inquiry impossible, ultimately making true, authentic dialogue impossible, which ultimately makes lasting relational and collective healing impossible.

When we're beating ourselves up for not thinking and speaking perfectly, our capacity to listen energetically to others with an open mind and an open heart becomes harder and harder. We start to listen only for the words. Our minds become consumed with assessing whether the words spoken are the right ones or the wrong ones. Whether they're reflecting the right values or the wrong ones. And as soon as we're in that state, our interactions with those who are different from us can only result in diminishment, rejection and exclusion. No matter how high our ideals, if we can't be ourselves, and if people feel essentially unsafe being who they are in our presence, we cannot transform this world into one where people are treated and honored with equal reverence. We can only create new, increasingly specialized and differentiated versions of the same old crap.

No one's *Integrity* can discover itself and flourish in an environment riddled with division. True *Integrity* understands, at the core of cores, there is no separation within us, or between us.

Before I bring my reflections to an end, I want to acknowledge something I've noticed in all of the people I know who've spent their lives working within the fields of reconciliation, mediation, diversity awareness and healing historic wounds. They're all very different people, but one quality they all share is an ability to hold a safe space for extremely honest conversations. Where everyone is invited to put their worst thoughts, fears and biases on the table. Where ignorance is not judged as a horrible, unforgivable thing that needs to be nipped in the bud, put on trial or shoved in the closet. It's seen as a universal experience that all of us share.

Our shared ignorance is our first common ground. When a group of people can begin a dialogue with that humbling realization, it can begin to practice real listening.

So there you go. You've got some of my personal thoughts on the *Wisdom Keeper* of *Equality* and *Tenderness*.

Now let's invite you to explore some of your own!

PRACTICAL INVITATIONS TO EXPLORE MORE DEEPLY

Feel free to write your responses down in your journal. If other questions arise for you, answer them too—instead. Trust yourself. These are just prompts to get you started.

QUESTIONS FOR CONTEMPLATION

Is there a part (or more than one part) of yourself that you've been refusing to love?

Feminene -list

What is it, or what are they?

What have you tended to see as a *Weakness* in you? What quality or struggle of yours brings u the most shame, is hardest to share with others or talk about?

Can you find its inherent strength? (If you can't find it on your own, I encourage you to explore this questio with someone that you trust deeply. If you don't have someone in your life that you trust deeply enough t explore this with, it may be time for you to find such a person. Ideally, it will be someone you consider to b a true *Wisdom Keeper*, the real deal. It may be a therapist, mentor, healer, clergy, shaman, circle holder o social worker. It may be a friend or family member that you trust, but you just haven't dared to share thi deeply with yet.)

Can you embrace the inherent worth of all people equally? Even people who are very different from you?

Even people whose beliefs or behaviors you find deeply disturbing? In what situations do you find this to be especially challenging? In political or social justice situations? In your nuclear or extended family? Think about the people in your life with whom you most strongly disagree or feel judged or misunderstood by. What would it take to truly see them as part of your human family? (We're not talking about liking, prioritizing or spending time with/on everyone equally. We're talking about something much deeper than that. We're talking about the kind of *Loving-Kindness* that lives in the heart, regardless of who we're with or where we are. We're talking about a *Tenderness* for humanity that can be embodied energetically … and as a result of that subtle embodiment, can change our world for the better.)

d honest look at what you're finding funny these days. When are you truly being etting off steam?

e you using humor effectively, to speak a truth that needs to be spoken? And when are you just an? Notice when you're taking something political and making it personal. Are there any ways in ur attempt to deal with fear, exhaustion, exasperation, desperation and disillusionment might be harm? When you're not sure, you might want to ask yourself, "How might I feel if someone thought omething like that about me? Or about my body? Or my family members? Or my friends? etc."

r *Tenderness* with someone who could really use it today—a person with whom it ily. As you do so, notice how you genuinely show your *Tenderness*. Through words, aze, a smile, a lift in your eyebrows?

think of someone in your personal/professional life with whom you have a hard time ith?

n't have to be the person you have the *hardest* time dealing with—just someone whose attitudes, beliefs aviors can really get under your skin. Come up with one simple act of kindness you could do today in n to this person. Make sure that it's doable, and honest. Don't go overboard. There needs to be a n amount of resonance, congruity and authenticity within the action for it to be worthwhile. Ask elf the question, "Given the nature of this relationship and this situation, what's the most tender thing I o?" In some cases, your act of kindness might be *not to act on an impulse*. For example, if the relationship to be outwardly contentious, your best act of kindness might be to simply refrain from reacting the way usually do during a conversation. You might have to get very creative here. Have a good laugh while e coming up with ideas. What matters is that you make a conscious choice, that your act of kindness is ational. (This is more about you and where you're coming from, than about what comes of what you do.)

could show *yourself Tenderness* today (in your personal journal, with a friend, in a small in your everyday life), what would you do?

at needs to happen inside of your own body, breath and thinking mind for you to actually feel *Tenderness*?

WHO INSPIRES *LOVING-KINDNESS* IN YOUR PERSONAL WISDOM WHEEL?

Now it's time for you to choose the *Wisdom Keeper* who will sit in your **Wisdom Wheel**, in the position of *Loving-Kindness*.

I encourage you to choose this card with eyes closed, and allow the powers of synchronicity to work for you … unless you have a very strong feeling that there is a particular *Wisdom Keeper* who needs to be in this position. If that's the case, go for it!

Spread your cards out face down. You can shuffle them first if you like. These are big cards, so you may have to be creative in how you shuffle. Make sure you have your journal close by.

Before you pick your card, close your eyes.

Resting one or both hands on your heart. Inside or out loud, in your own words, ask for the right *Wisdom Keeper* to come to you.

Say something like, "I am calling upon you, *Wisdom Keeper*, to hold the space for *Loving-Kindness*. I welcome you and trust that you are exactly the *Wisdom Keeper* I need to teach me how to feel, receive and practice *Loving-Kindness* in my life, and in my relationships."

Then reach down with your hand, and either feel the cards … or hold your hand above the cards, and feel the energy of the cards.

Let one call you, and pick that one.

Once you have your card, place it FACE UP on the East Side of your Wheel, the seat meant for the *Wisdom Keeper* of *Loving-Kindness*.

PRACTICAL INVITATIONS TO EXPLORE MORE DEEPLY

NOTE: If you decided to leave the *Wisdom Keeper* of *Equality* and *Tenderness* in your deck, and you've pulled it for your **Personal Wheel of Integrity**, this likely means that—when it comes to *Loving-Kindness*—the personal and collective are especially interconnected for you these days. I encourage you to already begin to notice how the people around you are embodying *Loving-Kindness*, or NOT doing so. Ask yourself, how might what's going on in the collective be mirroring something going on inside of you?

If you've drawn a different *Wisdom Keeper* than the one I pulled, find the *Wisdom Keeper* of *Equality* and *Tenderness* in your deck, and place this card right next to the *Wisdom Keeper* you pulled for the seat of *Loving-Kindness* on your **Personal Wheel of Integrity**. Allow these two *Wisdom Keepers* to hold the archetype of *Loving-Kindness* and a resilient heart together. In your contemplations, conversations and journaling, I invite you to let your own *Imagination* help you uncover possible areas of thematic synergy between the two. Enjoy paradoxes where you find them!

GET TO KNOW YOUR PERSONAL WISDOM KEEPER OF
LOVING-KINDNESS

Before you look in the Inner Guidebook, I invite you to spend a little time looking at your *Wisdom Keeper*. If their eyes are open, look into their eyes.

If not, gaze upon the face with a soft gaze and a soft heart.

Allow your eyes to drift around the face, taking in the symbols.

Allow your heart to engage even more deeply with the *Wisdom Keeper*.

Notice how this *Wisdom Keeper* makes you feel.

Now look at the number and the word on the card. Does this number or this word have a special association for you? Regardless of what's in the book? What is it? Just make a note in your mind or in your journal. No need to hold onto it.

QUESTIONS TO EXPLORE

Here are some simple questions for you to explore on your own, to help you connect even more deeply with this *Wisdom Keeper* who has been called to sit in the seat of *Loving-Kindness*. Feel free to write your responses down in your journal. If other questions arise for you, answer them too—or instead. Trust yourself. These are just prompts to get you started.

Remember: This is just the beginning of your relationship with this *Wisdom Keeper* sitting in the seat of *Loving-Kindness*. Even if you don't fully understand why this *Wisdom Keeper* came to you, or why it picked this particular position on your Wheel, it is the perfect one for you. Its mission will be revealed over time, as long as you stay open to it and engage with an inquiry of the heart.

- How do you experience *Loving-Kindness* in this *Wisdom Keeper*?

- If you were to sit down and have a conversation with this *Wisdom Keeper*, how do you think their *Kindness* would be expressed? (e.g., Through touch? Through words? Through an expression in the eyes? Through sharing knowledge? Through ceremony? Through a physical gift? Through a mantra? Through concrete advice? etc.)

- Is there something about this being that could bring out the *Loving-Kindness* in you? If it's possible to describe it, what is that something? Are you willing to allow this 'opening to *Kindness*' to happen? What does this particular kind of *Loving-Kindness* feel like … in your heart? Your body? Your breath? Just notice. Jot down any insights that come. Take this subtle feeling out into the world today and see what happens.

- If this *Wisdom Keeper* had a single, simple message for you about *Loving-Kindness*, what would it be? Write it down on your **Integrity Wheel** where your *Wisdom Keeper* sits.

DIVE INTO THE BOOK

Take out your book and find the page that corresponds with your *Wisdom Keeper* at the seat of *Loving-Kindness*.

At your own pace, do the following:

1. Read Richard Rudd's quote. Look at the Shadow, Siddhi and Gift words that are connected to this *Wisdom Keeper*, inspired by *The Gene Keys*.

2. Allow your mind to add the word *Integrity* to the mix. Play with these various combinations and allow insights to emerge. (e.g., "The *Integrity* of Kindness," "*Tenderness* expressed with *Integrity*," "*Tenderness* that lacks *Integrity*," "Weak *Integrity*," "*Integrity* that embraces *Weakness*," "The *Integrity* of *Equality*," "*Equality* without *Integrity*," etc.)

3. Read the story of your *Wisdom Keeper*, then the Gift for You Section.

4. Remember, as shared in our Initiation Module, the *Wisdom Keepers* are unique individuals with their own life experience. Your *Wisdom Keeper* has come to understand the nature of the Gift, Shadow and Siddhi (or spiritual essence) that they carry, in their own way.

5. You don't have to relate to the story of your *Wisdom Keeper* right now. You may relate to certain aspects of it, and not others. This is just one story of how one being came to experience a shadow, embody a gift and connect with a spiritual essence. Your story is yours, equally rich, equally fascinating, equally full of potential.

6. Look through the Questions for Contemplation in the Inner Guidebook. Perhaps one or two will open up a door for you. See whether any of the questions in particular connect you to the theme of *Integrity*.

7. Jot any insights, questions or doodles down in your journal.

8. If you are familiar with *The Gene Keys*, this particular *Wisdom Keeper* may correspond with a Gene Key that you have in your profile. Allow what you know about this Gene Key and its unique placement in your profile to creatively synergize with the themes of *Integrity*, *Loving-Kindness*, *Tenderness*, *Weakness* and *Equality*. See what happens!

SHARE WITH OTHERS

I invite you to share your experience with this *Wisdom Keeper* with a friend, partner or inside of a small group of trusted people. Let your fellow explorer(s) know which *Wisdom Keeper* called you and has taken its place at the seat of *Loving-Kindness*. Take turns sharing whichever aspect of your journey you've found most inspiring, challenging or interesting. Share from your journal or simply from your heart.

Make sure that you create a safe space where you and others know that whatever you share will be held confidential, as well as respected. You might want to come up with basic sharing and listening guidelines to be sure that everyone feels safe, or visit the ones shared in the Initiation Module.

PARTNER EXERCISE #1:
EMBODYING LOVING-KINDNESS WITH ANOTHER

Sit facing your partner. Make sure each of you know which *Wisdom Keeper* is sitting in the seat of *Loving-Kindness* in each of your **Wheels of Integrity**. Decide who will be reading first and who will be listening first.

Reader: Read the 'Gift to You' out loud for your partner. When you are reading, genuinely open your heart and infuse your voice with *Loving-Kindness*.

Listener: While you are listening, do your best to not only hear the words that are spoken, but to receive the *Loving-Kindness* emanating from your partner.

Reflect on the experience together, each of you sharing how it felt to read out loud from a place of *Loving-Kindness*, and to receive a message from someone who is emanating *Loving-Kindness*.

Switch roles and go through the process again.

Go to page #34 for **Simple Guidelines for Sharing** and **Listening**.

EXERCISE #2:
A LOVING-KINDNESS MEDITATION
(This can be done alone, with a partner, or in a small group.)

Body Position

Close your eyes. Sit comfortably with your feet flat on the floor and your spine straight. Relax your whole body. Keep your eyes closed throughout the whole visualization and bring your awareness inward. Without straining or concentrating, just relax and gently follow the instructions.

> Take a deep breath in. Hold your breath for four seconds.
> And breathe out for four seconds.
> Do that again.
> Take a deep breath in. Hold your breath for four seconds.
> And breathe out for four seconds.
> Do that three more times …

Receiving *Loving-Kindness*

Keeping your eyes closed, bring back into your awareness the *Wisdom Keeper* of *Tenderness* and *Equality*. See their face … and the kindness in their eyes. Imagine them standing just to your right, looking upon you with *Tenderness*. Feel them sending you love. Unconditional love. Feel them sending you wishes for your safety … for your well-being … and for your happiness. Sense their embracing of you as part of their human family, just as you are. Without having to change a thing. Feel their warm wishes and love washing over you like a warm, soothing breeze.

Now bring to mind the *Wisdom Keeper* who sits in the seat of your **Personal Wheel of Integrity**. Imagine that person standing on your left side, looking upon you as someone they deeply cherish. Feel this *Wisdom Keeper* sending you wishes for your wellness … for your health … and for your happiness. Feel their *Loving-Kindness* and warmth flowing towards you, washing over you. Feel yourself relaxing into this gentle stream of unconditional love. Knowing that you are safe.

Now imagine that you are surrounded by all of the people who love you and have ever loved you ... truly. All of the people you can remember who've treated you with *Loving-Kindness*, with *Tenderness*. Who've spoken to you as an equal, as if you belonged here in this world. Take some time to picture these people, these friends and loved ones surrounding you.

See them standing around you, at just the right distance from you so that you feel supported but not overwhelmed. And feel them sending you wishes for your happiness, your well-being, your health, your safety. Bask in this open field of warm wishes and love. Feel yourself being filled up and overflowing with *Loving-Kindness*.

Sending *Loving-Kindness* to Loved Ones

Now picture a specific person that you love, perhaps a relative or a friend. This person, like you, wishes to have a happy life. Send warm wishes to that person.

If it feels right, in your mind, say silently ... three times:

"May your life be filled with happiness, health and well-being."

Sending *Loving-Kindness* to Neutral People

Now think of an acquaintance, someone you don't know very well. You may not have any particular feeling towards this person at all. Acknowledge in your heart that you and this person are alike in the sense that you both wish to have a good life.

Now send all of your wishes for well-being to that person. If it feels right, repeat silently ... three times: "Just as I wish to live with ease and happiness, I also wish for you to live with ease and happiness."

Bring another acquaintance into your mind, another person who you feel relatively neutral towards. It could be a neighbor, or a colleague, or someone else that you see around but do not know very well. Just like you, this person also wishes to experience joy and well-being in his or her life.

Now send all of your good wishes to that person. If it feels right, say silently to yourself:
"May you be happy, may you be healthy, may you be free from all pain."

Sending *Loving-Kindness* to Difficult People

Now think of someone in your life who you've experienced as difficult or challenging. Imagine them sitting before you, at just the right distance so that you feel safe yet present with this person. Notice if anything changes in your breathing, or in your heart … or solar plexus … or belly. Stay connected to your breath. Keep relaxing and letting go. Let go a little more.

Remind yourself of your *Wisdom Keepers* and the people who love you, who are surrounding you with *Loving-Kindness* and unconditional love. Feel their love helping you to relax even more. See if you can feel gratitude in your heart for that love and support. Allow that gratitude to flow through your body and breath, like a warm gentle light.

Now acknowledge in your heart that you and this person sitting before you are alike … in the sense that you both wish to have a good life. That's all. Simply acknowledge that you share a wish for a good life. You have that in common.

Now send wishes for well-being to that person. If it feels right, repeat silently … three times:

"Just as I wish to live with ease and happiness, I also wish for you to live with ease and happiness."

Sending *Loving-Kindness* to All Living Beings

Now take a deep breath…
Keep a gentle smile on your face…
Allow yourself to fully become a *Wisdom Keeper* of *Loving-Kindness*…
Open to your breath, into your heart.
Feel your heart expand easily and effortlessly
Bring your breath all the way down to your belly.

Now expand your awareness and picture the whole earth in front of you.

See our planet as a beautiful glowing ball of blue light, like a pearl … sprinkled with billions of living beings—human beings, animals, plants, mountains and trees.

From the depth of your open, relaxed heart of *Loving-Kindness*, send your warm wishes to all of the living beings on this pearl of beauty, on our planet earth, who, just like you, want to be happy: "Just as I wish to live with ease, happiness and good health, may you live with ease, happiness, and good health. May you be safe and free of pain."

Take a deep breath in. And breathe out. And another deep breath in and let it go.

When you're ready, you may open your eyes.

Notice the state of your mind and how you feel after this meditation.

In your own time, jot down any thoughts or feelings that came up for you in this meditation.

Share them with someone you trust.

Be open to bringing this state out into your day, in a subtle, gentle way.

See what happens.

EXERCISE #3:
THE INNER SMILE

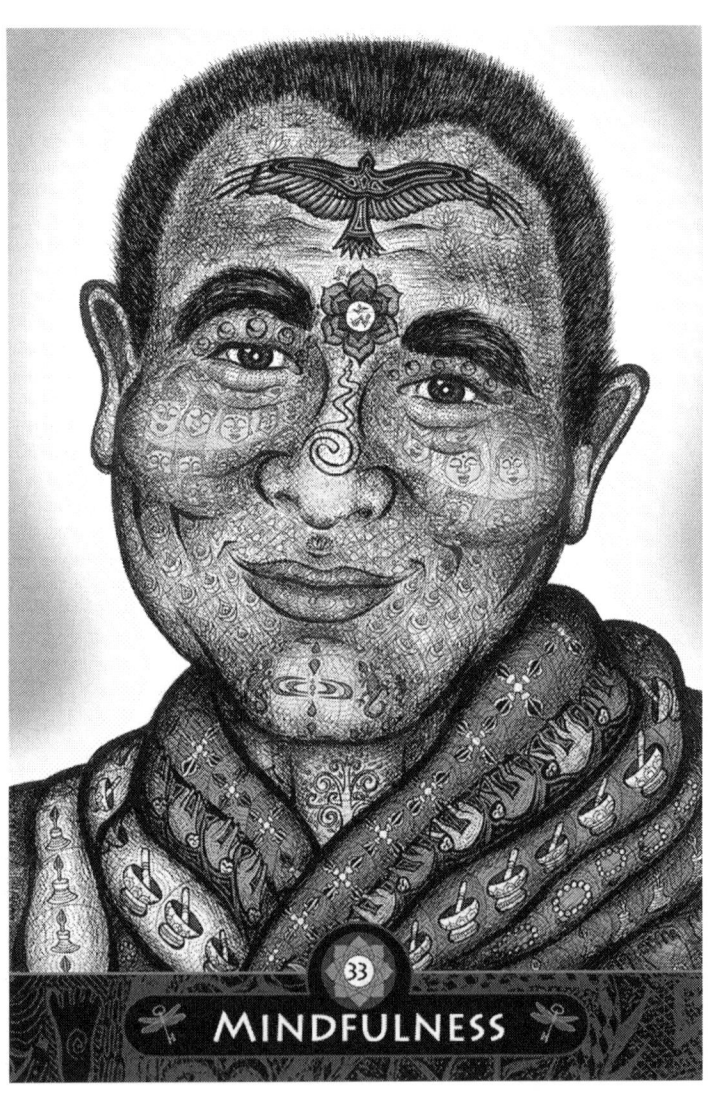

33

MINDFULNESS

The 'inner smile' is a well-known Taoist Neidan practice. While I wasn't consciously thinking about this practice when drawing the *Wisdom Keepers*, I can see now that almost all of the *Wisdom Keepers* are master practitioners of the Inner Smile!

Traditionally, the Inner Smile is directed to each of the body's major organs (or a chosen body part in need of attention). The purpose of this practice is to activate an energy of *Loving-Kindness* throughout the body and a profound experience of healing. Normally, one engages in this practice while sitting down in a calm place where it's easy to focus. I totally recommend that.

In service of the **Wisdom Wheel of Integrity**, however, I'd like to invite you (me too!) to experiment with bringing this practice out into the world, and into our relationships.

Can we call in the Inner Smile more spontaneously, when we really need it—like when we're with people or in environments where *Loving-Kindness* doesn't come easily? That's what I'm inviting here.

Here are a few Inner Smile prompts to remember during those challenging relational moments:

Wherever you happen to be, whether you're standing or sitting, bring your attention to your spine. See if you can allow it to naturally become just a bit more upright. As you bring more subtle alignment to your body, feel your head, neck and throat relax.

Take two or three slow, deep breaths. Relax your belly. Be just a little more present.

Place the tip of your tongue gently on the roof of your mouth, allowing it to relax just behind your front teeth.

Smile gently, letting your lips spread to the side and lift up just slightly. Feel your face relaxing as you do this.

If you can, bring your awareness to your Third Eye. Feeling a subtle stream of warm energy gathering there. Allow a part of your awareness to rest right in the center of your head, where the pineal gland lives, what the Taoists call the 'Crystal Palace.'

As this energy gathers, feel your eyes naturally smiling. Allow the spirit of *Loving-Kindness* to flow through your eyes, no matter who or what is in your line of vision.

Take another deep breath. Remind yourself that the *Loving-Kindness* flowing through your eyes out into the world around you is also making its way into your own body, bringing healing energy wherever it's needed.

MODULE THREE

"I cannot conceive of a greater loss than the loss of one's self-respect."

~ Mahatma Gandhi

WISDOM KEEPING WORDS

Valerie Creane, PsyD
Psychotherapist & Spiritual Director

"We often think of integrity related to how we interface with the world—whether we are honest and honoring our values when interacting with others.

It's important to also consider how we manifest our integrity in relation to ourselves.

Do we treat ourselves with the honesty, care and respect with which we treat others?

As a therapist (and ever-evolving human!), I have found that perhaps our greatest challenge is learning to love and respect ourselves, including trusting our inner authority."

WHAT IS *HEALTHY SELF-RESPECT?* AND WHY IS IT NECESSARY TO *INTEGRITY?*

In our last module, we looked at the importance of *Loving-Kindness* and the essential role it plays in living a life with *Integrity*. We may have the best values and highest principles in the world. But if we're not decent people, what's the point?!

In this module, we're going to be looking at a quality that is equally important to *Loving-Kindness* when it comes to *Integrity*. I'm referring to the quality of *Healthy Self-Respect*. When we have *Healthy Self-Respect*, we have the ability to set healthy boundaries. When we can set healthy boundaries, we are able to care for ourselves, and we are free to effectively care for those around us.

It can be helpful here to think of our **Wisdom Wheel of Integrity** like a system of checks and balances. Each council member is here to contribute to the overall balance of the whole.

A strong moral code—without *Loving-Kindness*—can manifest itself through a shadow of Meanness. Similarly, *Loving-Kindness* without *Healthy Self-Respect* can un-healthfully manifest itself through the shadows of people-pleasing, self-sacrifice and codependence.

The majority of people who are drawn to the healing arts or various forms of social/spiritual activism (or to a course like this one!) … are kind-hearted, sensitive and compassionate people.

If you're anything like me, you probably tend to feel best when things are harmonious—both outside of you and inside of you.

But the thing is that life is rarely harmonious. And it's certainly not harmonious all of the time.

When I was growing up, there was a lot of love in my family. But it was not harmonious! Not by a long-shot. We had lots of sweet moments, but we also had PLENTY of challenging, painful dynamics that were anything but comfortable. I learned very early on not only to be a peace-seeker but a peace-maker. And I wouldn't be surprised if some of you taking this course can relate.

Of course, if the world didn't have inner and outer peace-makers, we'd all be in deep trouble. We need peace-makers and agents of diplomacy and kindness to help us build bridges, get along, communicate better, understand and forgive each other, so that we can all live in as much harmony as possible.

Still, *Loving-Kindness* junkies like myself tend to run into problems when our deep desire for peace is driven by an even deeper fear of conflict—which is often hiding beneath an even deeper fear of anger.

In a book I wrote over 25 years ago that I recently published, *Walking a Fine Line: How to Be a Professional Wisdom Keeper in the Healing Arts*, I wrote about how I used to think if I was just peaceful, loving and kind enough, things would work out.

And whoa, was I wrong! Although it is wonderful when being nice is enough to make something good happen in a relationship, or in the world, being a 'good person' isn't always enough. At some point, if we want to live in *Integrity*, many of us *Loving-Kindness* addicts have to face a tough but essential truth:

Sometimes in life, even nice guys have to be bad guys—especially when being perceived as a 'bad guy' is experienced as taboo.

I've found in my own life, if I continue to cling to my goodness, I can end up using harmony-loving philosophies to justify my own passivity. I can use it to justify an unwillingness to stand up for myself and my core values. Sometimes my fear of conflict makes me miss out on chances to stand up for people who are in real need of my advocacy (not just people, but our whole planet and all of its inhabitants!).

Many of us whose emotional or childhood survival strategies involved an over-identification with *Loving-Kindness* end up choosing our goodness … over our own well-being. We just can't stand the thought of someone perceiving us as aggressive, selfish, stubborn, impolite, hurtful, overpowering, dominating, intimidating, pig-headed, irrational, rebellious … you get the idea.

Unfortunately, when we stick with 'Loving-Kindness' at all costs, we risk abandoning who we truly are, sitting on our authentic power and biting our truth-telling tongues. In our deep desire to be good, or at least to always be seen as good, we can actually end up doing a lot of bad. We can do plenty of bad to ourselves, putting ourselves in abusive, disrespectful and disempowering situations.

And, even if it's the last thing we want, we can do some bad in the world. It's not that we intentionally go out there and do bad things. It's more like we unintentionally let bad things happen because we're too afraid of what might happen if we stand up and insist on something else happening. Or, we apply a sweet bandage here and there, but we don't really address the root cause of anyone's suffering.

Again, when it comes to *Healthy Self-Respect*, I'm not encouraging you or anyone to be mean, insensitive or heartless. I'm encouraging you to sometimes do what is required in order to be true to yourself, to take care of yourself, to be true to a virtue you hold dear, or to courageously address a collective need that is valid.

As I'm sure you know, sometimes lobbyists have to be pushy in order to get a good law passed. And while many of our most impactful human rights movements did have roots in spirituality, where *Loving-Kindness*, *Equality* and compassion were deeply valued, most effective human rights movements didn't gain traction because protestors took to the streets with protest signs saying, "Please" and "Thank You."

So, this *Wisdom Keeper*, this *Integrity* Council Member is here to remind us of the fact that sometimes, very nice people have to be stubborn, determined, loud, annoying, confronting, boundaried or frustrating in order to honor themselves, and in order to get through to those around them so that they can manifest their essentially loving and kind ideas.

It is in the spirit of balance that I now call upon the *Wisdom Keeper* who will sit on the opposite side of *Loving-Kindness*, and who will make their home in the Collective seat of *Healthy Self-Respect*.

Let's see who comes to us!

WHO SITS IN THE COLLECTIVE SEAT OF
HEALTHY SELF-RESPECT?

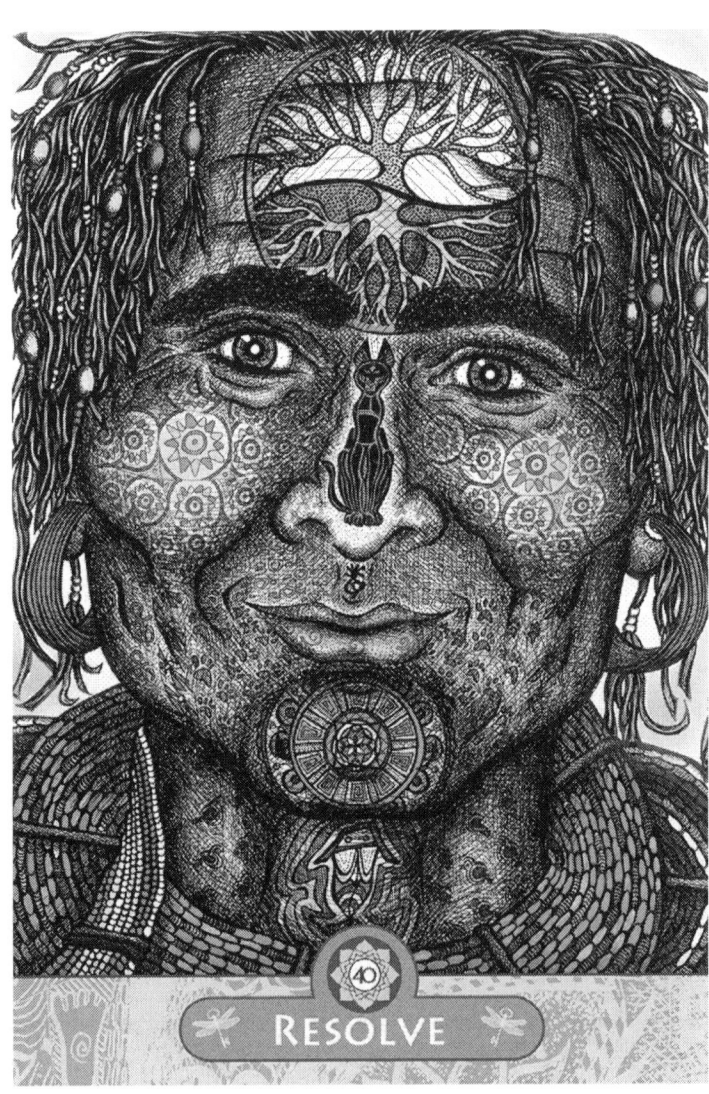

"The 40th Gift of Resolve is about becoming adept at giving to yourself. Ultimately, it is about deep physical relaxation."

~ Richard Rudd

Gift: *Resolve*
Shadow: *Exhaustion*
Siddhi: *Divine Will*

The *Wisdom Keeper* I pulled on behalf of the collective, the *Wisdom Keeper* who shall be sitting in the seat of *Healthy Self-Respect*, is the *Wisdom Keeper* of *Resolve* and *Divine Will*. This is such a good card for what we're exploring here. It speaks straight to the fact that the true Revolution must begin within, from a place of deep inner relaxation, self-honoring and an ability to set healthy boundaries.

So, let me start by sharing the story of this *Wisdom Keeper* with you, and then their Gift to You. After that, I'll share some reflections that came up for me in relation to this *Wisdom Keeper*, and some ways for you to explore your own inner response to the collective *Integrity* themes inherent in this *Wisdom Keeper*'s story.

As with the first *Wisdom Keeper* story, get comfortable, relax and listen deeply with your heart.

MY WISDOM STORY

I was born into a family with spiritual and artistic traditions that went back thousands of years. But as a boy, I was stolen from my parents and forced into slavery. My master had nothing but contempt for me. He saw and treated me like an animal. I survived by giving of myself tirelessly, without complaint. When beaten for not working hard enough, I worked harder.

Because of my obedience and unusual strength, I was given increasing amounts of responsibility, thus stress. Eventually, my stomach started to burn, and my digestive system shut down. I got so sick and exhausted my master no longer had use for me. He threw me out, with nothing but the scars on my back.

A young woman found me in the dirt. She was dark-skinned like me, but she was free. She gave me shelter, nursed me back to health and found work for me. I didn't mind the low pay or invisibility. I acquiesced in my role willingly—grateful not to be beaten. For many years, I worked very hard. But I was lonely, broken and deeply afraid of people. I only drew comfort from carving statues out of wood, like the ones my grandfather made before I was taken away. One day the woman saw my carvings and was impressed. She encouraged me to set up shop for myself. I said 'no,' but she was stubborn and intuitive.

The next thing I knew, she purchased a small shop and hung up a sign with my name on the door. For the first time in my life, I was my own boss. This realization brought forth an ache so vast that I cried myself to sleep for a year.

As I embraced my pain, I grew to love what I did. It was hard work, but it didn't feel like it. My shop thrived, my stomach healed and my body grew young again. Eventually, I let the woman into my heart, and she became my wife. It took us ten years to save up enough money to return to our homeland and start a new life.

The moment my foot stepped on African soil, I looked up at the open sky, inhaled the sweet air, and my entire being relaxed. Then I heard the distant sounds of my people singing and drumming, waiting for us to join them. I looked into the eyes of my beloved and knew I was home.

MY GIFT TO YOU

I come when it is time to relax, and for you to understand the importance of balancing your desire to serve the world and your need to enjoy your life. Do not be afraid to stand your ground, set healthy boundaries or be generous with yourself. Your time and energy are precious. Sometimes saying 'no' to the right thing can be more powerful than saying 'yes.' I'm not asking that you rest now and then. I want you to relax, deeply and fully, with your whole being. When you are genuinely relaxed, you are free to work in harmony with your true nature and environment, and will have all of the energy required to complete any task, no matter how great. The health of our communities and nations depends on people who have true inner *Resolve* and a balanced physical, emotional and spiritual life.

REFLECTIONS

There is so much I love about this *Wisdom Keeper* and his powerful story. While I can't possibly know the unimaginable suffering he's experienced—having been stolen from his home, forced into slavery and violently abused for much of his childhood and adult life—there is so much I have learned from him, and continue to learn. And though our lives have obviously been very different, there is also a lot that I can relate to. I'm guessing you can too.

For example, you and I may not have ever been enslaved, but that doesn't mean we don't know what it's like to feel powerless, or stripped of our dignity or sense of personal agency. Perhaps there was a time in your life when you felt like you had no choice other than to obey orders, follow the rules or get in line. Perhaps you've had a parent, a boss, a teacher, a partner or someone you were deeply dependent on who was intimidating, manipulative, abusive or controlling in some way. Abuse can be subtle but still extremely damaging.

Maybe there have been times in your life when you've had to do work or take on jobs that you hated. Maybe you've had to sacrifice dream after dream, just to pay the bills, and you could see no other option for yourself. Maybe that's happening right now!

You may also be someone whose strengths, good will, talents and abilities have landed you with way too much responsibility. Maybe you've learned that you can handle a whole lot of responsibility, but you still haven't learned that just because you CAN doesn't mean you have to. Or maybe you know that you don't have to carry so much responsibility, but you don't know how to stop. Or you don't feel you have the right to say 'no.' Or maybe you're terrified that if you do say 'no,' everything will fall apart, or people will get angry, or someone else will have to take on the burden you've been carrying and you'd never be able to forgive yourself for leaving such a heavy burden with someone else.

Or maybe you've become addicted to stress. Maybe you wouldn't even know what to do with yourself if you weren't busy all the time, if you weren't filling your hours and days with giving and overextending yourself. Maybe deep down, you're afraid to be alone, or to be bored, or to be replaced, or to feel pain, or to feel lost, irrelevant or utterly purposeless.

And, so you're willing to keep saying 'yes' and 'yes' and 'yes' at the expense of your body, and at the expense of your health, and at the expense of your own *Healthy Self-Respect*. You've become your own cruel task master, not listening to your body's cries for help, or even if you do hear them … you constantly override them.

Maybe like this *Wisdom Keeper*, you've experienced your share of heartburn and digestive issues, or deep *Exhaustion*. Maybe you've suffered from chronic fatigue, insomnia, hormonal imbalances, skin disturbances, back pain, or some other illness that feels somehow connected to a deep level of stress. Or burnout. If you're honest with yourself, you'll probably know which of your body's symptoms are at least partially related to burnout and stress, and an inability—or unwillingness—to slow down.

Only you know how your personal story relates to the story of this particular *Wisdom Keeper*.

However yours or mine does, what matters is that we hear and truly receive his main message for us. This *Wisdom Keeper* is telling us that it's not only OK to have a self; he's telling us that it is essential. Even if we're working for someone else, we still—in the end—need to be our own boss, or our bodies will suffer. Our minds will suffer. Our emotional systems will suffer. Our spirit will suffer.

In a very profound way, we are all being called home, just like this *Wisdom Keeper*. Our health depends on it. Our *Integrity* depends on it.

One extremely important thing that this *Wisdom Keeper* is telling us is that *Healthy Self-Respect* is deeply connected to Self-Care. That our Inner *Resolve* is intimately dependent on our ability and willingness to Relax … at a very deep level. He's not talking about sitting down and watching Netflix for twelve hours a day over the weekend (not that there isn't a time or place for good entertainment!). He's talking about something much more profound than that. The kind of relaxation that truly nourishes the soul.

For the *Wisdom Keeper* of *Resolve* and *Divine Will*, ultimately, truly relaxing meant reclaiming a part of his ancestral heritage, finding a way to drop into a deeply surrendered, present state of being through the creative process.

This part of the *Wisdom Keeper*'s story reminds me of a client I once had (one I could relate to!). She was an extremely busy social worker, counselor and activist. She worked in the heart of the inner city, and was surrounded by so much suffering. She witnessed one heart-wrenching example of injustice after another. After years of relentlessly serving others through her therapeutic work and social change activities, her body finally gave out. She became overwhelmed with pain and *Exhaustion*.

Together we explored possible ways for her to slow down, and to nurture herself. But it wasn't easy. She had to work VERY hard on giving herself permission to NOT work so hard. This was a woman who'd done many *many* difficult things in her life. But slowing down was probably the hardest thing she'd ever have to do.

There were so many layers of guilt and fear for her to work through, as she considered being gentler with herself. She was afraid of betraying her clients and her colleagues. She was terrified of letting down her parents who'd always expected so much from her, and her extended family that had a humanly impossible work ethic. She felt guilty about abandoning her deepest values. She worried that if she took care of herself, that would mean that she'd be retreating into a life of privilege … while others in the world—who didn't have the options that she had—would still be suffering so much. She wasn't sure how she'd ever forgive herself for that.

But over time, she came to see and embrace her humanness. And she ended up having to face the fact that when she was this burned out, her over-extending and self-sacrificing tendencies didn't do anyone any good. She couldn't inspire anyone when she was exhausted, bitter, in pain and filled with resentment. And even though she wished she could, and Lord knows she tried, there was no way for her to effectively and genuinely transmit love and respect to anyone when she had no clue about how to love and respect herself.

Thankfully, just like this *Wisdom Keeper* of *Resolve* and *Divine Will*, this woman eventually found ways to relax. One of the activities that became one of her favorites was one that her great-grandmother had taught her when she was a little girl. Her family was Asian-American, and although she had completely assimilated into modern life in the U.S., her grandmother had taught her how to do Chinese calligraphy in her early years. She had forgotten all about it until one day she found herself walking home from an art shop with a calligraphy set under her arm. The next thing you know, she and her nervous system were completely entranced by a slow, delicate, meditative arts practice that had been passed down through the generations right into her lap. A deeply healing process took place as her life came back into greater balance.

So, maybe you and I aren't meant to carve statues out of wood, or move to Africa, or practice Chinese calligraphy. But maybe there is a place or a practice that is waiting to be discovered by us. Maybe there's a way for us to experience greater balance in our lives. And maybe a focus on *Healthy Self-Respect* holds the key to that transformation.

If I've learned anything over the years (as a counselor and a recovering co-dependent), it's that true healing occurs when there is an energetic balance between the giver and the receiver. Each person involved in a healing, teaching or philanthropic exchange may give or receive something very different. On the surface, it may very well look like one person is doing the giving and the other person is doing the receiving. But that doesn't matter. What matters is that the exchange leaves both parties feeling nourished and enlivened, not depleted and resentful. Resentment can be subtle. It can pop up when we least expect it. Even if we're good at convincing ourselves that we can survive on personal 'good will' alone, in the end, when deep down we feel like we're giving more than we're receiving, we end up subtly sending out a martyr-like message, "You owe me one!" It's rare that people are empowered through a relationship that feels riddled with debt.

So many of us who tend to value *Loving-Kindness* and workaholism over *Healthy Self-Respect* end up chronically putting up with situations that in the end aren't sustainable or good for anyone. It's so important that we learn that it's safe to have and express a 'self' in our personal and working relationships. Being selfless and overly-flexible can really sabotage our ability to genuinely connect with people, and to see them and their needs accurately.

I've also had many experiences where I've been confronted with the fact that a LOT of my hard work and attempts at offering *Loving-Kindness* to others wasn't received, wanted or needed anywhere as much as I thought it was … or as much as I needed it to be!

And that's the key, right there. "My *Loving-Kindness* wasn't needed as much as I NEEDED IT TO BE." I'd like to take a little more time to explore that statement—at the risk of being redundant. Because this 'need to be needed' is one of the main reasons why many of us who have struggled with co-dependency throughout our lives will have a very hard time fully receiving and respecting the gift of this *Wisdom Keeper*. It's also why we won't be able to fully embody *Healthy Self-Respect*, which is absolutely integral to living a life of *Integrity*.

First of all, let me make it clear that I'm not talking about healthy manifestations of Interdependency. We all need each other on this planet. Humans, animals, plants, insects, soil and sun alike. We're all interconnected. And without a willingness or ability to depend on each other and be depended on, we'd all be in big trouble!

What I'm talking about here is unhealthy levels of dependency, where we end up getting lost in self-sacrifice, people-pleasing, conflict-avoidance and over-exertion. And where our intimate relationships, social relationships, professional relationships and our entire way of engaging with the world around us suffers … because of our need to be needed, or of a fear of what will happen if we don't constantly meet the needs of the beings around us.

In *Walking a Fine Line*, I talk about how many professional *Wisdom Keepers* (whether they be therapists, healers, urban shamans, priestess circle holders, tarot card readers or yoga teachers) easily fall into the Martyr Trap. The same goes for people who are committed to social and planetary change.

In my own life, I've had phases where social-sacred activism has played a particularly big role. Over the past few years, (in addition to my work as a counselor, writer, teacher and artist … and my life as a mom, friend and community member), I've found myself becoming increasingly engaged in social issues—both in my own country and abroad.

My increased involvement with a Ugandan human rights organization, at a time when the humanity-loving work of my Ugandan colleagues put their lives in grave danger, has been especially challenging for me. It has forced me to take a good hard look at the often cruel and unjust limitations of the world we're living in, and at my own utterly human limitations. It's also forced me to deal with deep personal wounds that stem from my past.

Because of the violent and hostile climate of Uganda towards my dear friends and colleagues (who are basically people who work tirelessly to serve, love and protect the rights and lives of marginalized people), I found myself living in a constant state of fear that something horrible would happen to my Ugandan friends, people for whom I have so much love and respect.

Because of my personal history, I've always tended to carry an over-exaggerated sense of responsibility for the people around me. But this time, I really believed that if I didn't do absolutely everything in my power to ensure that they had the support and security they needed to survive this frightening time, they could be arrested (even executed) by a hostile government, abused by the police or brutally murdered in the streets. Even though my rational mind knew that there was only so much I could do, that I have absolutely no background or expertise in the realms of politics or global activism, and that we were up against the horrific and historical results of colonialism, deep-seated and institutional forms of discrimination, and a government system full of corruption, this time … saying 'no' or setting healthy limits didn't feel like an option. Even if my efforts didn't bring about lasting or effective change, a decision to put a boundary around what I could or would do felt unforgivable.

No matter what toll the situation took on my physical or emotional health, or on my family's financial and relational well-being, setting limits or practicing self-care didn't feel like an option for me. I just wasn't able to turn away … and I didn't know how to stay open-eyed, open-hearted and say 'no' at the same time.

One thing that made it feel especially impossible to set limits was that setting healthy limits or practicing self-care didn't feel like an option for my colleagues in Uganda either. If they didn't do everything they possibly could to deal with the situation, they wouldn't only be putting their own lives at risk, but the lives of the countless people they served and felt responsible for. So, they gave every ounce of themselves in an attempt to save lives and change the attitudes of leaders who were attempting to legalize persecution and violence against marginalized people. And, in order to do their work and to grow an exponentially growing amount of needs, they turned to me and others here in the States to support their efforts. How could I possibly say no? What they were to experience was a million times worse than anything I could imagine. The bravery, stamina and selflessness I witnessed in them was beyond inspiring.

But the truth (and the problem) was that—while our circumstances were different—all of us were being stretched beyond our energetic, financial and emotional capacity. We had all become well-intentioned yet exhausted victims of a hopeless, unjust and bigger-than-any-of-us situation. We were cogs in an endless wheel of suffering and unmet needs.

And for quite some time, none of us were willing to be the ones to say, "You know what? I can do *this*, but I just can't do *that*. Someone else is going to have to step in to take that one on. And, if no one does, then I'm going to have to tolerate the pain of knowing that so much of this situation is beyond my control, and that sometimes on planet earth, horrific things happen to really *really* good people."

I'll tell you what! There's something about trying to solve problems in Third World countries that can really humble a person.

Things got to a point where sacred activism had basically taken over my life. I had no boundaries. "Self-care" had been re-banned from my vocabulary. My health, relationships and ability to focus on my own life's work became so compromised that I could no longer ignore it. I noticed that I wasn't just having trouble setting limits around what I could do in relation to Uganda, I was having trouble setting limits everywhere. I was walking on a field of eggshells. All of the hard work I'd done in my life to heal unhealthy codependency tendencies had flown right out the window.

And as much as I like to think of myself as a kind and loving person, I was starting to resent it … big time. Because I looked around and noticed plenty of other people saying 'no,' exercising their bodies, reading good books, prioritizing their work, exploring their passions and taking vacations. Some people who were close to me didn't seem to have a problem saying 'no' to me during my moments of intense need, or making sure that they had the time and space they needed to take care of their own needs.

I also noticed that some of the people I was working so hard to hear and whose needs I was working so hard to honor (so that our work in Uganda could be effective) weren't necessarily seeing, appreciating or making use of my hard-labored contributions. Some of what I was doing was helpful. But some of it, for many reasons, just plain wasn't. The fact that a good chunk of my hard work wasn't actually being recognized, received or experienced as effective was extremely important for me to face. Talk about a hard pill to swallow.

It was noticing my overall ineffectiveness, as well as the stark and brutal contrast between what I was willing to do for others, and what I was willing to do for myself, that provided me with a big wake up call. I needed to take a deep breath and return to my own healing process. I needed to take a hard look at some of the painful childhood patterns and survival strategies that were being activated by this difficult situation. If I truly wanted to be of service in this world, if I wanted to be truly present, I had to deal with those childhood wounds that left me feeling so willing and in a hurry to abandon myself in order to be there for others.

The inner child in me was calling out for my *Loving-Kindness*. This was the child who'd learned from birth that the only way to secure her own safety and protection was by meeting the needs of the people around her, by making sure that nothing and no one fell apart. If she could just make sure that her parents, sister, family, community, THE WORLD were physically, emotionally and spiritually safe, then maybe, just maybe they'd be stable and 'surplussed' enough to take care of her. This inner child had lost all trust in other people. She'd also lost trust in the Universe itself. And when you don't trust people, and when you don't trust the Universe, there is no such thing as recognizing and surrendering to *Divine Will.*

Of course, the situation in Uganda and other equally cruel and horrible situations happening all over our world (even right in our own backyard) are very real. People all over our world are suffering; they are victims of real tragedies—both human- and nature-made. So, I'm not saying that difficult situations like the one I'm describing are just opportunities for privileged Wisdom Seekers to heal our codependency wounds. Or that surrendering to *Divine Will* means you passively sit by and watch horrible things happen to good people.

Painful situations are also wonderful opportunities for all of us to wake up, join the planetary family and get involved. These are opportunities for us to discover that much of the time, when we surrender our personal will to something much greater than ourselves, we end up just naturally, authentically, healthfully doing a lot of good.

But if we don't take an honest look at where we're coming from when attempting to make the world a better place, we may end up unconsciously or unintentionally making the world a worse place. In the name of empathy, sympathy and generosity, we end up adding stress, suffering and martyrdom to the human soup. And that's not good for anyone.

Slowly but surely, I'm learning that during those moments when my personal will is aligned with *Divine Will,* my generous, loving acts feel nourishing to me, not draining. They feel authentic, not forced. I feel called by love, not guilt, obligation or fear. My contributions are full of creativity, not drudgery. This doesn't mean I'm not working hard, or facing challenges, or acknowledging my very real limitations. But it feels different in my bones, in my heart. Just like the *Wisdom Keeper* of *Resolve* and *Divine Will* says, "It was hard work, but it didn't feel like it."

I'd like to invite you now to take a look at some of the Practical Invitations to Explore More Deeply. There are some exercises for you designed to help you glean the wisdom from this *Wisdom Keeper*'s life experience and to relate it to your own life.

WISDOM KEEPING WORDS

Karin von Daler, REAT, MPF
Clinical Psychologist, Creative Arts Therapist, Self-Care Artist

"It was only when I decided to stop asking books and stars for advice but to listen to my soul that I really began to heal.

Self-healing is something quite different from therapy and treatment, which is more often about others telling you what you need or even what is wrong with you.

Self-healing is also not so much about doing something, but about letting go and opening yourself up to inspiration, to the very life force that flows through you and everything else.

Self-healing is about coming home to yourself and hearing what your body and soul are saying to you."

PRACTICAL INVITATIONS TO EXPLORE MORE DEEPLY
A CODEPENDENCY EXPLORATION

Here's a Codependency Exploration. If you find yourself saying 'yes' to more of these questions than you sense might be healthy, take it as a sign that you're in the right place! The seat of *Healthy Self-Respect* is likely one that has been beckoning you for quite some time. I encourage you to really dive deep into the Questions for Contemplation and Exercises offered in this Module. Your *Integrity* is depending on you!

- Do you find it difficult to make decisions in your relationships?

- Do you often look for or value other people's approval more than your own?

- Do you worry about being left or abandoned if you don't do what others expect or need you to do?

- Is it hard sometimes to identify what you're truly feeling?

- Do you struggle knowing and asking for what you need in your relationships?

- Do you often second-guess yourself or have trouble trusting your own instincts?

- Do you tend to feel super responsible—not only for your own actions but the actions of others?

- Do you sometimes feel overwhelmed by the suffering in the world around you?

- Does taking care of yourself often fall to the bottom of your to-do list?

- Is it hard for you to say 'no' and to set healthy limits?

- Have you experienced being very dependent on other people, even in relationships that you know weren't good for you?

THE KARPMAN DRAMA TRIANGLE

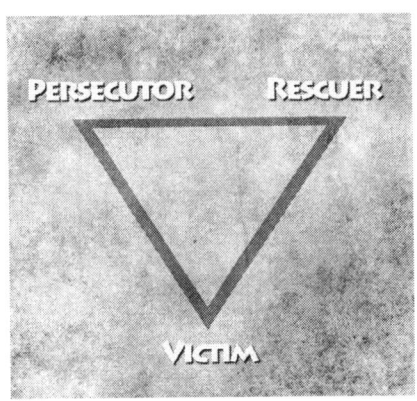

Stephen Karpman, M.D., a student of Eric Berne (considered the father of Transactional Analysis), conceived of a social model called the Karpman Drama Triangle in the early 70s. This model maps out conflict- or drama-laden relational interactions and shows how unhealthy codependent patterns often play out between people. I have found this model to be enormously helpful and clarifying in my personal life, as well as in my professional work as a counselor.

Although I can't do complete justice to the model here, I'd like to share a bit about it so that you can explore it further if you feel moved to do so. When it comes to learning *Healthy Self-Respect*, self-responsibility, self-assertion and other-empowerment, this is a fantastic tool for insight and growth. (Go to the Resource Section to find Karpman's website and learn about other inspiring publications of his.)

In the Drama Triangle, there are three positions (or "faces of drama") that people tend to assume. Most of us tend to gravitate towards one of the three positions. Most often, our primary (or habitual) role in the Triangle reflects the one we needed to play in order to survive our childhoods. However, if we're self-observant, we find that things are much more nuanced than we'd like to think! We may find ourselves landing in certain positions around certain people, or in very specific circumstances. It's not unusual, especially during charged interactions, that we find ourselves rotating through all three positions … at rapid speed. Every position has a hidden agenda and a self-serving payoff. No matter which role we fall into, we are not acting from a self-responsible or genuinely altruistic place.

We all fall into these patterns. It's very human!

The more we are able to cultivate self-awareness in the moment, the more we can benefit from this model, learn how we contribute to codependent dynamics in our relationships, and how we can break unhealthy patterns that no longer serve us.

Here are the three positions or stances in the Triangle, and the qualities they represent:

Note about the Victim: When the word *Victim* is used, it doesn't necessarily mean that someone is an actual victim of a situation. It means that the person is feeling like, identifying as or acting like a victim. Take my friends in Uganda. They are actually—objectively—being victimized by a corrupt and cruel government. But most of the time, they don't identify as or act like Victims. Similarly, many people who act like bullies actually feel like victims. Then they use their inner experience of being persecuted to justify their abusive and oppressive behaviors. So, things aren't always what they seem.

The Victim...

- Holds a basic stance of "Poor Me!"

- Feels stuck, indecisive and acts from a place of powerlessness

- Feels unloved, under-prioritized and persecuted

- Feels helpless, trapped, like they have no choice or ability to change their circumstance

- Refuses to hold themselves accountable

- Avoids responsibility, blames others and expects to be rescued by someone else

- Gets their needs met through guilt-tripping, sympathy-seeking and manipulative behaviors

- Holds a 'one-down position'

The Persecutor (a.k.a. Villain)...

- Holds a basic stance of "It's all your fault!"
- Is often angry and frustrated
- Blames, shames, criticizes, teases and patronizes others
- Has to be right, at any cost
- Is rigid, controlling, self-righteous, intimidating, vindictive and authoritarian
- Sees the world as full of winners and losers
- Acts from a place of anger, resentment and a sense of entitlement
- Does not know how to collaborate with others
- Holds a 'one-up position'

The Rescuer (Caretaker)...

- Holds a basic stance of "Let me help you."
- Feels an enormous pressure to step in and come to the rescue
- Plays the martyr, enabler and co-dependent
- Needs to be needed, thus keeps the *Victim* dependent on them
- Has learned to get love and approval through self-sacrifice and helping
- Is over-protective and conflict-avoidant
- Focuses on others' needs, worries and problems in order to escape their own
- Has a deep-seated sense of guilt and inadequacy
- Feels like their entire self-worth is dependent on their ability to help others
- Is often self-neglecting, overwhelmed, burdened, overworked and exhausted
- Holds a 'one-up position'

Now that I've described the Drama Triangle, I'll share a few questions for you to explore.

DRAMA TRIANGLE QUESTIONS FOR CONTEMPLATION

Which would you say is your Primary Position, the role you most often find yourself playing?

What are the qualities that you can most relate to? Are there any of the qualities associated with your Primary Position that you don't (or no longer) relate to? What are those? Why do you think that is?

How might your early experiences (as a fetus, baby, toddler and young child) have led to this becoming your Primary Position?

How did becoming or acting like a Persecutor, Rescuer or Victim help you to survive? To get your needs met? What might have happened to you (or those you loved) if you didn't play this role? Can you offer yourself some *Loving-Kindness* here?

Think of a very uncomfortable or heated interaction you've had in your life, one where you definitely played this Primary or habitual role.

See if you can remember the details of what happened. Be as honest with yourself as possible. Try to identify the moment when you felt most triggered. What or who triggered you? What was it about the content or tone of what was said that pushed your button? If you could come up with a simple statement that accurately reflects the most charged part of what you heard (not necessarily what was said), what would it be? What was the message that kicked you into your habitual position? (For example, "It's all your fault." Or, "No one cares about me. I'm all alone." Or, "Let me take care of this. I don't want you to worry anymore." You get the idea. Take as much responsibility for what happened during that interaction as you can. Own the part of you that contributed to or amplified the dysfunction. When, in the conversation or interaction, did you end up playing out (internally or externally) the other two positions? As you explore this experience, be open to your empathy—for yourself and others—growing.

SUGGESTIONS FOR PRIMARY POSITION TRANSFORMATIONS

From the *Victim* of circumstance to the *Creator* of your own reality

Shift your focus from what you *don't* want to what you *do* want.

Keep a Gratitude Journal (start to track everything that's actually going well in your life).

Take full responsibility for what you think, how you feel, and what you do.

Remind yourself that you have a magnificently creative *Imagination* and that you're perfectly able to solve your own problems.

Make *Healthy Self-Respect* and Self-Care your top priorities.

Every time you find yourself looking to someone else, hoping they'll solve your problem, ask yourself, "What do I want? What are three simple steps I can take to provide myself with what I want?"

From the *Persecutor* to an *Assertive Challenger*

During heated interactions, see if you can find a gracious way to leave the room and give yourself a little break. Take a few deep breaths and see if you can relax your body. Once you're in a safe, quiet place, and your nervous system has calmed down a bit, ask yourself why it is that you're so angry? What is upsetting you the most or causing you to react so strongly? Where do you feel most powerless or trapped? Does anything about this situation remind you of a time when you were a child? A time when you were blamed or criticized? Or a time when you had to be strong and unswayable in order to protect yourself or someone else? Or a time when you saw and spoke the truth and were punished for it? Can you identify a deeper want or a need in yourself? How can you respect yourself, set a boundary or ask a challenging question while still being kind?

Learn to tell the difference between healthfully challenging someone, and blaming, criticizing or oppressing them. Ask someone you truly trust for honest feedback. Let them help you learn about your impact on people and how small adjustments to your behavior can make a big difference. Ask yourself, "Am I being fair right now?" It's OK to be firm, but it's also important that you are being fair. This means you have to take other people's perspectives into consideration when looking at a situation, along with your own.

From *the Rescuer* to *the Empower-er*

Think of a time when you tried to rescue someone or fix their problems for them and things ended badly. What was going on in this person's life? What gave you the impression that you needed to step in and come to the rescue? (e.g., Were you asked directly? Did you volunteer?) What were you afraid might happen if you didn't take responsibility for fixing the situation? What ended up happening? In what ways were your efforts disempowering—for yourself, for others? What was the most important lesson you learned from that experience?

Think of someone in your life (not a child) who—if you're honest with yourself—is unhealthfully dependent on you? In what ways have you encouraged this dependency? Where don't you fully trust their ability to take charge of their own lives? Where might you not trust in your own ability to survive their not needing you quite so much? What are you most afraid of? (e.g., To discover that you're not worthy of love? To be alone? To lose your 'good person' identity?) If this person were to suddenly discover their own power and agency, (and need you less), what might you be afraid of? Think of one thing you could do (or stop doing) that would help move each of you closer to a stance of *Healthy Self-Respect* and self-responsibility.

Think of a time when you didn't run to someone's rescue, but you were still able to have a positive and empowering impact? What happened? How did you approach this person and their predicament? What kind of support did you offer? (e.g., a resource, some information, some coaching advice, empowering questions for them to solve their own problems, etc.) What did you *not* offer? How would you say the person was ultimately empowered by your interaction? How were you empowered by the way you showed up? What gave you the courage to practice self-restraint … and *Healthy Self-Respect?*
In relation to which relationship or life arena do you have the hardest time setting a boundary? Where do

you feel most burned out, resentful or jaded? If you were to set a boundary, what would it be? What holds you back? If you were somehow miraculously able to say 'no,' what would you do with all of the time and energy you'd be freeing up? Perhaps you can't pull the plug on the entire relationship or activity right now. Perhaps you can't commit to going on a three-month-long vacation. But what healthy boundary *can* you set? What self-nourishing activity *could* you do? Make a commitment to yourself to set one boundary and do one nice thing for yourself.

ADDITIONAL QUESTIONS FOR CONTEMPLATION & OPEN CONVERSATION WITH TRUSTED PEOPLE

- Where (with whom) do you find it most difficult to set a limit? What are you afraid of?

- Where are you not valuing yourself and your precious energy?

- What (or who) in your life exhausts you?

- If you truly respected yourself, what would you do differently? What would you start doing much more of? What would you stop doing all together?

- Have you learned how to enjoy your solitude?

- Are you getting enough alone time? What truly relaxes you?

- Do you keep others at a distance because of painful experiences?

- Have you ever felt your inner *Resolve* aligned with *Divine Will?*

- Allow yourself to say "no" to someone or something today. Write your reflections in your journal.

- Think of a person in your life that embodies *Healthy Self-Respect?* Someone who is able to balance self-care with a compassionate and collaborative nature? If you were to emulate them in one concrete (and doable) way, what would you do?

- Take a moment to think of a place or a landscape that speaks deeply to your soul. A place you've been where you felt deeply nourished, at home and at peace. Imagine yourself there. If you're inspired, make a "Coming Home to Myself" collage, full of imagery that helps your shoulders to relax and heart open to yourself.

WHO INSPIRES *HEALTHY SELF-RESPECT* IN YOUR PERSONAL WISDOM WHEEL?

Now it's time for you to choose the *Wisdom Keeper* who will sit in your **Wisdom Wheel**, in the position of *Healthy Self-Respect*. I encourage you to choose blindly, and allow the powers of synchronicity to work for you … unless you have a very strong feeling that there is a particular *Wisdom Keeper* who needs to be in this position.

Spread your cards out face down. You can shuffle them first if you like. These are big cards, so you may have to be creative in how you shuffle. Make sure you have your journal close by.

Before you pick your card, close your eyes, resting both hands on your heart. Inside, or out loud, in your own words, ask for your *Wisdom Keeper* to come to you. Say something like, "I am calling upon you, *Wisdom Keeper*, to hold the place of *Healthy Self-Respect*. I welcome you and trust that you are exactly the *Wisdom Keeper* I need to teach me how to feel, receive and practice healthy boundary-setting in my life."

Then reach down with your hand, and either feel the cards … or hold your hand above the cards, and feel the energy of the cards. Let one call you, and pick that one.

Once you have your card, place it FACE UP on the left side of your Wheel, the seat meant for the *Wisdom Keeper* of *Healthy Self-Respect*.

PRACTICAL INVITATIONS TO EXPLORE MORE DEEPLY

NOTE: If you decided to leave the *Wisdom Keeper* of *Resolve* and *Divine Will* in your deck, and you've pulled it for your **Personal Wheel of Integrity**, this likely means that—when it comes to *Healthy Self-Respect*—the personal and collective are especially interconnected for you these days. I encourage you to already begin to notice how the people around you are embodying *Healthy Self-Respect* and setting healthy limits, or NOT doing so. And ask yourself, how might what's going on in the collective be mirroring something going on inside of you?

If you've drawn a different *Wisdom Keeper* than the one I pulled, find the *Wisdom Keeper* of *Resolve* & *Divine Will* in your deck, and place this card right next to the *Wisdom Keeper* you pulled for the seat of *Healthy Self-Respect* on your **Personal Wheel of Integrity**. Allow these two *Wisdom Keepers* to hold the archetype of *Healthy Self-Respect* and *Resolve* together. In your contemplations, conversations and journaling, I invite you to let your own *Imagination* help you uncover possible areas of thematic synergy between the two. Enjoy paradoxes where you find them!

GET TO KNOW YOUR PERSONAL WISDOM KEEPER OF
HEALTHY SELF-RESPECT

Before you look in the Inner Guidebook, I invite you to spend a little time looking at your *Wisdom Keeper*. If their eyes are open, look into their eyes.

If not, gaze upon the face with a soft gaze and a soft heart.

Allow your eyes to drift around the face, taking in the symbols.

Allow your heart to engage even more deeply with the *Wisdom Keeper*.

Notice how this *Wisdom Keeper* makes you feel.

Now look at the number and the word on the card. Does this number or this word have a special association for you? Regardless of what's in the book? What is it? Just make a note in your mind or in your journal. No need to hold onto it.

QUESTIONS TO EXPLORE

Here are some simple questions for you to explore on your own, to help you connect even more deeply with this *Wisdom Keeper* who has been called to sit in the seat of *Healthy Self-Respect*. Feel free to write your responses down in your journal. If other questions arise for you, answer them too—or instead. Trust yourself. These are just prompts to get you started.

Remember: This is just the beginning of your relationship with this *Wisdom Keeper* sitting in the seat of *Healthy Self-Respect*. Even if you don't fully understand why this *Wisdom Keeper* came to you, or why it picked this particular position on your Wheel, it's the perfect one for you. Its mission will be revealed over time, as long as you stay open to it and engage with an inquiry of the heart.

- How do you experience the boundaries of this *Wisdom Keeper*?

- If you were to sit down with this *Wisdom Keeper*, and you were full of needs or feeling helpless and hopeless, how do you imagine they would balance their kindness with healthy boundaries? How would they express their boundaries? Would they do it with words? With action? With energy? Through sharing knowledge? Through an arts process? Through ritual? Through a physical gift? Through a mantra? Concrete advice?

- Is there something about this being that could teach you about having and setting healthy boundaries?

- If this *Wisdom Keeper* had a simple message for you about self-care, what would it be?

- Is there something about this being that invites out the *Healthy Self-Respect* in you? If it's possible to describe it, what is that something? Are you willing to allow this 'opening to self-honoring' to happen within you? What does this particular kind of *Healthy Self-Respect* feel like … in your heart? Your body? Your shoulders? Your jaw? Your solar plexus? Your aura? Your breath? Just notice. Jot down any insights that come. Take this subtle feeling out into the world today, and see what happens.

- If this *Wisdom Keeper* had a single, simple message for you about *Healthy Self-Respect*, what would it be? Write it down on your **Personal Integrity Wheel** or your journal.

DIVE INTO THE BOOK

Take out your book and find the page that corresponds with your *Wisdom Keeper* at the seat of *Healthy Self-Respect*.

At your own pace, do the following:

1. Read Richard Rudd's quote. Look at the Shadow, Siddhi and Gift words that are connected to this *Wisdom Keeper*, inspired by *The Gene Keys*.

2. Allow your mind to add the word *Integrity* to the mix. Play with these various combinations and allow insights to emerge (e.g., "The *Integrity* of (Gift)," "(Gift) expressed with *Healthy Self-Respect*" "(Gift) that lacks *Integrity*," "(Shadow) of *Healthy Self-Respect*," "*Integrity* that embraces (Shadow)," "The *Integrity* of (Siddhi)," "(Siddhic quality) without *Healthy Self-Respect*," etc.).

3. Read the story of your *Wisdom Keeper*. Then the Gift for You Section.

4. Remember, as shared in our Initiation Module, the *Wisdom Keepers* are unique individuals, with their own life experience. Your *Wisdom Keeper* has come to understand the nature of the Gift, Shadow and Siddhi (or spiritual essence) that they carry, in their own way.

5. You don't have to relate to the story of your *Wisdom Keeper* right now. You may relate to certain aspects of it, and not others. This is just one story of how one being came to experience a shadow, embody a gift and connect with a spiritual essence. Your story is yours, equally rich, equally fascinating, equally full of potential.

6. Look through the Questions for Contemplation in the Inner Guidebook. Perhaps one or two will open up a door for you. See whether any of the questions in particular connect you to the theme of *Integrity*.

7. Jot any insights, questions or doodles down in your journal.

8. If you are familiar with *The Gene Keys*, this particular *Wisdom Keeper* may correspond with a Gene Key that you have in your profile. Allow what you know about this Gene Key and its unique placement in your profile to creatively synergize with the themes of *Healthy Self-Respect*, self-care and *Integrity*. See what happens!

EXERCISE FOR YOU:
MAKE A SELF-CARE VOW

Feel free to use the following prompts if they're helpful. Or make up your own. I suggest starting simple. You may ultimately want to focus on one or two areas. Make this as manageable as possible. Once you get started on a self-care journey, it gets easier to keep going!

In relation to my Body, I will practice self-care by…

_____.

In relation to the contents of my Mind, I will practice self-care by…

_____.

In relation to my Creative Spirit, I will practice self-care by…

_____.

In relation to my Inner Child, I will practice self-care by…

_____.

In relation to my Friends and Family, I will practice self-care by…

_____.

In relation to my Professional Life, I will practice self-care by…

_____.

In relation to my Community or Social Change work, I will practice self-care by…

_____.

In relation to _____, I will practice self-care by…

_____.

SHARE WITH OTHERS

I invite you to share your experience with this *Wisdom Keeper* with a friend, partner or inside of a small group of trusted people. Let your fellow explorer(s) know which *Wisdom Keeper* called you and has taken its place at the seat of *Healthy Self-Respect*. Take turns sharing whichever aspect of your journey you've found most inspiring, challenging or interesting. Share your Self-Care Action plan from your journal, your contemplations or anything you feel inspired to share from your heart.

Make sure that you create a safe space where you and others know that whatever you share will be held confidential, as well as respected. You might want to come up with basic sharing and listening guidelines to be sure that everyone feels safe.

PARTNER EXERCISE #1:
EMBODYING SELF-RESPECT WITH ANOTHER

Sit facing your partner. Make sure each of you knows which *Wisdom Keeper* is sitting in the seat of *Healthy Self-Respect* in each of your **Wheels of Integrity**. Decide who will be reading first and who will be listening first.

Reader: Read the 'Gift to You' out loud for your partner. When you are reading, breathe deeply into your belly, relax your shoulders and straighten your spine. Allow a genuine feeling of respect and regard for yourself to infuse your voice. Read assertively.

Listener: While you are listening, do your best to not only hear the words that are spoken, but to receive the *Healthy Self-Respect* emanating from your partner. Even more importantly, embody your own *Healthy Self-Respect*. Just like the reader, relax your shoulders and allow your spine to unfurl upwards, and your head and neck to align with the rest of your upright body. Feel what it's like to listen to someone while respecting yourself. How does it feel to be receptive and assertive at the same time?

Reflect on the experience together, each of you sharing how it felt to read out loud from a place of *Healthy Self-Respect* and to receive a message from someone who is emanating *Healthy Self-Respect*—while you yourself are feeling your own *Healthy Self-Respect*! Switch roles and go through the process again.

Go to page #34 for **Simple Guidelines for Sharing** and **Listening**.

"I'd rather be true to myself than be consistent."

~ Ram Dass

MODULE FOUR

"Being deeply loved by someone gives you strength, while loving someone deeply gives you courage."

~ Lao Tzu

"In the end, we will remember not the words of our enemies, but the silence of our friends."

~ Martin Luther King Jr.

WISDOM KEEPING WORDS

Mbali Marais
Global Medicine Woman & Initiated Stick Diviner in the Dagara Tradition

"When we enter into nature, we'll find the Law of Integrity.
It is the state of being whole, true to one's inner nature, one's medicine,
working together in unity for the good of the community.

For humans, all of this takes courage,
and trust that when we realize we are a part of a much bigger whole,
we belong and are better able to navigate a world which often says otherwise."

WHAT IS *COURAGEOUS SELF-TRUST?*
AND WHY IS IT NECESSARY TO *INTEGRITY?*

In our last module, we explored some of the problems we run into when we continually prioritize *Loving-Kindness* over *Healthy Self-Respect*.

We also learned that sometimes, in our efforts to bring ourselves back into balance (by practicing more *Healthy Self-Respect*, self-care and setting more healthy boundaries—which is not an easy task for many of us), we end up having to face some very painful truths.

One of the most difficult lessons we may learn is that sometimes horrible things happen to very good people and there's nothing we can do about it.

In this module, we're going to be looking at the theme of *Courageous Self-Trust* and how it relates to *Integrity*. One of the things we're going to look at together is another not-so-pleasant truth: When the quality of *Courageous Self-Trust* has not been sufficiently developed, essentially good people can end up doing very bad things. And I'm not just talking about unhealthy and personally disempowering things. I'm talking about hurtful, damaging and cruel things. I'll share more about this later. There's a big shadow lurking here.

It takes a lot to cultivate *Courageous Self-Trust*. For most of us humans, we find ourselves on a daily basis pulled in a million directions, often away from our own internal sense of what is right for us, or right in general. Without even realizing it, we take in and come to own the values, beliefs and habits of the people around us. We walk around with our parents, teachers, peers, bosses, institutions, cultural leaders, spiritual leaders, political leaders, fellow activists, even global trends speaking to us through 'shoulds' in our minds and on our myriad of screens. They're all telling us what to think, what to feel, what to need, what to value, what to do, and why *not* doing this or that would be a bad, even dangerous idea.

More often than not, the conditioning forces in our lives contradict each other, making our task of 'figuring out' what to do—or just plain trusting ourselves—even more difficult and confusing.

Of course, just as it is in our nature to have active crazy minds, it is in our nature as human beings to be influenced, to be penetrable. Our sensitivity and openness to the world around us is one of our most wonderful qualities. Without the nurturing and inspiring influence of others, few of us would ever reach our full potential as unique and yet interconnected human beings. And yet, when it comes to the cultivation of *Courageous Self-Trust*, we can get so lost. So 'under the influence' that we can't feel our truth or access our most authentic instincts at all.

For years, I studied, taught and ultimately wrote about a system called Human Design. Human Design was brought to the world by a man named Ra Uru Hu. It is an extraordinary system that weaves epigenetic wisdom together with the I Ching, Astrology, Kabbalah, the Chakra System and more.

Over the years, this system has been explored by countless people and has evolved into a rich tapestry of perspectives and approaches. Richard Rudd, the author of *The Gene Keys*—which lies at the heart of the *Wisdom Keepers Oracle Deck*—was a Human Design student and teacher for many years before his journey took him into more archetypal and mystical waters. Together with Werner and Laura Pitzal, he co-created Integral Human Design, which brings *The Gene Keys* and Human Design together in a fascinating way.

I have a deep appreciation for all three of these worlds. This is why I've dedicated a good portion of my adult life toward encouraging people to explore Human Design, The Gene Keys and the intersection between the two in a variety of creative, embodied and psychologically grounded ways. I've done this especially through my *Designed to Blossom* Self-Study Program and Books.

If you're interested in learning more about that aspect of my work, I'm happy to share some resources with you. For our purposes now, however, I'd like to share about one aspect of Human Design because I feel it carries particular relevance to our theme of *Courageous Self-Trust*.

In Human Design, there is a term called "*Authority*." What we call *Authority* in Human Design is that place we can turn to for Truth—that part of us that we can trust to make our decisions in life, and to honor our own right timing.

In the traditional Human Design world, not everyone has the same kind of *Authority*, so one person's decision-making process can look and feel much different from another's.

Just as an example: One person might be designed to rely on their intuitive 'hits' in the moment, while another might be designed to 'feel out' people, situations and opportunities over time before knowing who and what is right for them.

One of the greatest gifts of Human Design as a system or tool is that it puts each person in touch with their own unique truth-detecting system, so that in any given moment, they can make the most of the gifts they receive from the outside world without losing themselves, or their ground, in the process.

Personally, I've found Human Design to be a wonderful support, especially when it comes to cultivating the arts of authenticity and self-trust. That said, I don't believe Human Design is the only way for people to learn how to bypass the conditioned mind and trust themselves. It just happens to be an unusually practical system for self-development that focuses on authentic decision-making.

Whether we learn about our *Authority* through Human Design, or come to know our inner truth compass another way, learning how to truly trust oneself and act from a place of inner *Authority* is far from easy. It requires courage.

Courage often requires that we do things that don't make logical sense. That we trust something other than what's in our minds, and that we act in alignment with our true nature, our deepest intuition or our hearts. Courage sometimes asks us to go against our conditioning (whether from our early upbringing or current cultural influences). It asks us to do things that the people we care about—or the people whose respect we want—don't understand or approve of. When *Courageous Self-Trust* is more than a concept, and instead something we embody, we are able to move beyond flight-fright-freeze reactivity and become proactive players on our own life stage. We become servants of the one beating heart that connects us all.

So, it is in the spirit of proactive, loving *Integrity* that I now call upon the *Wisdom Keeper* who will sit in the Collective seat of *Courageous Self-Trust*.

Let's see who comes to us!

WHO SITS IN THE COLLECTIVE SEAT OF
COURAGEOUS SELF-TRUST?

"Ultimately, the only ones who will be given positions of control will be those who have given up being in control."

~ Richard Rudd

Gift: *Authority*
Shadow: *Control*
Siddhi: *Valor*

The *Wisdom Keeper* I pulled on behalf of the collective, the *Wisdom Keeper* who shall be sitting in the seat of *Courageous Self-Trust* over the coming days and weeks, is the *Wisdom Keeper* of *Authority* and *Valor*. How perfect that this is the card that comes to us now. The Gift of this *Wisdom Keeper* is actually called *Authority*!

So, let me start by sharing the story of this *Wisdom Keeper* with you, and then their Gift to You. After that, I'll share some reflections that came up for me in relation to this *Wisdom Keeper*, and some ways for you to explore your own inner response to the collective *Integrity* themes inherent in this *Wisdom Keeper*'s story.

Get a cup of tea and relax at your favorite reading spot. Ask your heart and soul to open up to receiving the wisdom, power and healing offered to you by this dear friend and ally.

MY WISDOM STORY

I was a trust fund baby. While my dad disappeared behind closed doors with business moguls and ruled the world, my mother ruled the household—with her perfectly manicured nails and social graces. As they raised me, they were controlling and critical, and I was submissive. I cringed at the way they treated our servants, whom I suspected secretly despised my parents as much as I did.

The moment I got my driver's license, I grabbed some cash and bolted, leaving my parents and my trust fund in the dust. I had no plan, no college education. All I cared about was being free of their stuffy, oppressive world. So I worked odd jobs, went with the flow and reveled in the fact that I no longer represented the imperious elite.

But when my financial cushion ran out, so did my sense of adventure. Too humiliated to beg my parents to take me back, I lived in my car behind our house, eating the food that was thrown away. One of the servants found me there and insisted on taking me in. Her family had almost nothing but gave me everything. I was grateful, and humbled. I realized how bitter and selfish I'd become, how deeply I resented my parents for their narrowness and selfishness, at society for ignoring the needy, and more importantly, at myself, for being too weak and pathetic to help myself, much less anyone else. I'd become as obsessed about money as my father, and as disconnected from the real world as my mother. If I truly wanted my life to be useful, I'd have to take responsibility for it.

From that point on, my heart took over. I became driven by a deep desire to give back to this family and to serve those in need. I got my act together, re-engaged with the world and eventually reconciled with my parents. Instead of rejecting their resources, I inspired them to recognize the humanity of the people who worked for them. My parents are now the biggest financial supporters of my efforts to give homes to the homeless, bring gardens to food deserts and represent people whose voices have not been heard. The more my heart opens, the more loyalty I inspire, in the most unlikely places.

MY GIFT TO YOU

I come to share that true power has nothing to do with money or control. True power is about speaking and acting from the heart, and grounding all that you do in a deep desire to serve. Becoming the true *Authority* in your own life requires both that you surrender and that you rise up to meet whatever life brings your way, with enthusiasm, gratitude and a deep sense of responsibility. You will know that you are owning your *Authority* when you inspire loyalty and connectivity wherever you go. When everyone you represent—no matter what role they play, feels empowered, impassioned and respected. It is time to listen deeply to the will of the groups in your life, and act sincerely on their behalf. It is time to become the trustworthy person I know you can be.

REFLECTIONS

This *Wisdom Keeper* is a wonderful one to sit in our collective seat of *Self-Trust*. He even was even born into this world as a trust fund baby! How wild is that!

This *Wisdom Keeper*'s story demonstrates how the road to *Courageous Self-Trust* can be a long one. It often includes more than one phase. As a young boy, this *Wisdom Keeper* was able to sense and see those places where his parents lacked *Integrity*. But he was not able to free himself from their control. He had to remain submissive and wait until he was old enough to drive before he could break free from the hold his parents, and their value system, had on him. Leaving the security of his childhood home, leaving his trust fund in the dust and rebelling against his authoritarian, powerful parents certainly required courage. In order to be true to himself, he had to be willing to disappoint people, to not be liked or approved of, and to lose the guarantee of a life of financial security.

His early years demonstrate how often, in the beginning of our development, *Courageous Self-Trust* often shows up as an ability to identify who and what we don't trust, to resist what feels wrong and to do whatever it takes to get out from under the control of both perceived and real external authorities.

But our *Wisdom Keeper*'s story doesn't end there. It shows us how, ultimately, true *Courageous Self-Trust* must go deeper and farther than instinctive rebellion.

As we mature, *Courageous Self-Trust* transcends the ability or willingness to be 'against' something. We have to discover what we're for and courageously stand for that. Often, just like this *Wisdom Keeper*, we need to encounter new role models who can show us a different way of being. Usually, the most inspiring ways of being are sourced in love, generosity and service, just like the servant who invited the *Wisdom Keeper* into her home and family with a generosity of spirit that far surpassed her family's material resources. Slowly but surely, we learn ways of being that are healthy for our nervous systems and mirror neurons. Ways that promote interconnectivity, collaboration, *Equality* and creativity, as opposed to fear, contraction, competition and *Control*. These ways also leave room for everyone's uniqueness, the sovereignty of individuals.

Once we find out that we can survive without the blessing of an external *Authority* figure, once we've found a safe place to be our true selves, once we've discovered others who truly love and inspire us … we can begin to stand courageously, authentically and compassionately for a cause or purpose that positively influences our surroundings. We still may be called to do things that require courage. We may still struggle with the fact that the majority of others don't understand what the heck we're doing. (I certainly know how that feels!) But our actions will be defined and driven by a deep inner 'yes,' not by a conflicted, tortured, rebellious 'no.' In the end, *Courageous Self-Trust* leads to a life of service.

As I shared earlier, when people are learning about Human Design, they are encouraged to enter into an experiment. A big part of that experiment involves daring to rely on a particular *Authority*, or truth compass. As we learn to approach the decision-making process with increased autonomy and freedom, accessing and honoring our *Authority* can be incredibly empowering.

However, embracing our *Authority* as defined by Human Design doesn't mean that we have to ignore or discard the many other ways we can access our knowing. We all have intuitions, feelings and gut responses. We all have body-intelligence and cognitive capacities. We all have the capacity to tune into invisible, subtle and cosmic currents. We all have the potential to reach out to wise people who know us well. All of these options are at our disposal when we enter into a decision-making process or a situation where we're being asked to trust ourselves deeply.

Years back, when Richard Rudd was having one of his contemplative deep dives into Human Design, he had a fascinating revelation. It involved *Authority* as well as a particular Gene Key (the one that corresponds to the *Wisdom Keeper* of *Dislocation*, *Orientation* and *Unity* in this deck).

Without overwhelming you with too many details, Richard discovered that inside of all of us lives a potential *universal Authority*—a way for all of us to access what I like to call our *Inner Wisdom Keeper*. It doesn't matter what our Human Design chart looks like, or whether we've ever heard of Human Design! Our ability to connect deeply with the potential and essence represented by this Gene Key allows us to make clear decisions that are intrinsically authentic and in harmony with the whole of the cosmos.

According to Richard, and I agree with him fully, it's all in the frequency. When we are driven by fear and caught in the *shadow* frequency, our decisions inevitably disconnect us from the whole; we end up dislocated from all of life. When we open our hearts to life, we just naturally orient ourselves through our decision-making process towards our highest potential, which can't help but serve Creation.

When we become deeply oriented in this way, we open ourselves up to a direct experience of Unity and Oneness. We no longer need to let our emotions, reactivity or conditioned monkey minds tell us what to do. We only do what is in the Tao of our True Nature, which is connected to all of nature. This is why, as Richard wisely points out, so many mystical teachings guide us with the simplest directive of all: follow your heart.

I don't know if you remember, but towards the very beginning of this module, I shared that a frightening *shadow* can appear when we haven't sufficiently exercised our *Courageous Self-Trust* muscles. This shadow is like a wrecking ball to *Integrity* in that it can make essentially good people do horrific things. I'd like to take a little time to explore this shadow. Given all that is happening in our world, how much exposure we all have to suffering, and how easy it is to go numb and unconsciously give our consent to all sorts of horrible things, an awareness of this shadow seems particularly important.

I'd like to start by sharing about a psychological experiment you may have heard of because it is so connected to the theme we're exploring. Back in 1961, in the basement of a building at Yale University, a social psychologist named Stanley Milgram conducted this experiment. The Milgram Experiment took place three months after the German Nazi war criminal Adolf Eichmann went to trial in Israel. It was essentially created to help us understand how the cruelty enacted in the Holocaust—by so many people—could be explained. Could it be so simple that all of the Nazi leaders, war criminals and their millions of accomplices were 'just following orders?'

Milgram's experiment was essentially a study of human obedience to *Authority* figures. The study participants were all men, with different levels of education and a wide range of occupations. Although the subjects were led to believe that they were participating in a completely different experiment, the actual experiment involved their being told to obey an *Authority* figure who instructed them to perform acts that went against their personal conscience. More specifically, they were instructed to give electric shocks to a person referred to as a 'learner.' The learner, of course, was an actor, and the shocks were not real. But the study participants didn't know that. They believed that the electric shocks they were administering were real, and that the pain inflicted on the 'learners' was equally real. In order to teach the learner, they were told to gradually increase the electric shocks to levels that (if they were real) would have been fatal.

The results of this experiment were terrifying. A disturbingly high number of participants obeyed the orders they were given, even when they saw the learners suffering and they themselves felt bad about what they were doing. The Milgram Experiment, and similar ones, were repeated around the world. The results were all consistent.

The current relevance of this experiment isn't hard to find. Just the other day, I was listening to a podcast on *This American Life* by Ira Glass. The episode was called "The Out Crowd" and it featured a story written by Molly O'Toole, a *Los Angeles Times* Reporter. (I'll share a link to the podcast at the end of this workbook, in the Resource Section, so that it's available to you.)

This show looked at the painful reality of what's happening on the other side of the U.S. border in Mexico right now, in the year 2019. I'm not saying that our country has always had an impeccable history when it comes to treating immigrants and asylum seekers respectfully, or living up to its reputation as a welcoming, inclusive nation. But if you've been following U.S. news lately, things have gotten much worse. If you follow the news, you've probably heard of the fact that children are being separated from their families, kept in cages and denied healthcare.

Now, because of our current administration's new asylum policy, an unprecedented number of migrants who are coming to the U.S. from all over the world in order to seek refuge (and who are attempting to go through legal channels) are also being sent back to Mexico.

Instead of being allowed into the U.S. in order to wait in safety for their immigration hearings (which had been common practice for a long time), they're now having to spend months and months living under extremely dangerous and inhumane conditions. In less than a year, since the current "Migrant Protection Protocols" were announced, over 60,000 asylum seekers have been pushed back across the southern border of the U.S.

When we hear statistics like this, many of us understandably nod our heads at (in this case) the U.S. government and imagine how terrible it must be for the people who have traveled hundreds of miles (often on foot, through treacherous terrains, with little resource and no support) in order to secure their and their family's safety, only to be thrown back into frightening conditions and unimaginable circumstances.

But we rarely take a moment to think about the fact that every single one of those 60,000 asylum seekers is not just being 'pushed back over the border' by some theoretical government with bad policies. These people and their families—most of them exhausted, traumatized and in complete darkness about the brutal and confusing process they're about to be put through—are being seen, heard and considered … and then separated from their loved ones, and most often rejected … literally 'pushed back into harm's way' … by actual human beings. By people like you and me.

The majority of the time, these asylum officers, these human beings, aren't bad people—although it can be easy to demonize them from a distance.

Asylum officers have hearts and a conscience. In fact, many of them are drawn to the profession because of their compassionate nature, because they want to play the role of welcoming people in need into their country. They want to be the people who can provide asylum seekers with a safe sanctuary, to demonstrate that there are places in the world where justice matters and all people are treated with respect and care. One of an asylum officer's central responsibilities is to make sure that no one gets returned to a home country that would put them in harm's way.

But in the case of the United States right now, (and as we know this sort of thing is happening all over the world), there's been a change of policy. And right now, our Southern border asylum officers' main responsibility is to keep people from coming into the country … as opposed to keeping them out of harm's way.

Before, asylum officers were encouraged to err on the side of leniency. If there was any concern that someone might be harmed, tortured or murdered if they were sent back to Mexico or their own country, the asylum officer was required to let them into the United States, where they could then wait safely for their case to be considered.

Now, the standards for proving that one is worthy of being let into the U.S. are impossibly high. If people can't name the particular person who might rape or kidnap them, or if they can't prove they'd been threatened specifically because of their nationality, or if they can't prove that the police would not protect them should they come in harm's way, or if they can't prove that anyone who has or might threaten them would be able to locate them, their asylum officers would have to send them back over the border.

Listening to this podcast, I learned that even people whose cases checked all of the required boxes, and whose asylum officers decided to keep them in the States, their cases were overruled by supervisors. This has happened time and time again. The statistics were kind of crazy. It was something like out of over 47,000 cases handled under the new policy, only eleven people were granted asylum or allowed to stay in the States.

So right now, hundreds of well-intentioned officers are finding themselves in a horrible predicament. If they want to keep their jobs, they have to do things that go against every *Courageous Self-Trust* cell in their bodies. They have to send people, even young children, into places where kidnappings, rape and violence against asylum seekers are well-documented.

I was so moved by this podcast and the opportunity to get to hear about what's happening at my country's borders from the perspective of asylum officers with a conscience. I learned that many officers are dealing with the situation by calling in sick, requesting transfers, retiring early and quitting. Like the younger version of our *Wisdom Keeper*, they are trusting themselves enough to know what they're against. They're 'getting out of Dodge.' That already takes courage.

One particular asylum officer's story, however, was particularly inspiring to me. I want to share it with you here because I feel he embodies a more matured version *Courageous Self-Trust* (and perseverance) that we're exploring together.

The man's name is Doug Stephens. Once he figured out what he was being asked to do as an asylum officer, (it didn't take him more than a couple of days to figure it out), he refused to do one more immigrant interview. Instead of calling in sick or requesting a transfer, he poured through all of his law books (luckily, he had a background in law) and came up with a long list of reasons why the new immigration policy was not only immoral, but illegal. Then he shared his concerns with his supervisors.

When his supervisors realized that he couldn't be convinced to just obey orders, they started disciplinary proceedings. Doug Stephens knew that he had no choice but to quit. But before he quit, he drafted a memo outlining all of the reasons he believed the new policy was illegal and why he was refusing to do the interviews. Then he sent the memo to everyone in the Citizenship and Immigration Services office in San Francisco and the two agency supervisors who were disciplining him. As a result of his action, absolutely nothing happened. His memo was completely ignored.

Most people would just call it a day at that point. But he didn't. Doug then sent the memo to his U.S. Senator. He also sent his resignation letter and the legal memo to everyone in San Francisco Asylum, about 80 people, and then to a representative for union officers all across the country. Then he walked out. No longer in government, this man is now working to draw attention to the program and encouraging others to speak out.

In the interview with him, he said something that I want to share with you here because it's so basic, but so profound.

"They make one change, and everyone at the office says, 'Oh, this is terrible, but we'll figure it out.' Then they make another change, and people say, 'This is terrible, but I need my job. I'm going to do it even if I don't want to. And I'll complain about the work; I'll complain about the hours. But at the end of the day, I'm gonna do it. And the more I do it, the easier it is to do.' And that is terrifying. That's how all the awful things in the world happen. That's how you get so many good people doing really bad things."

So here is the shadow again. In this case, we're talking about essentially good people sending asylum seekers back to their own country to get sick, hungry, unfairly arrested, kidnapped, raped or killed.

Clearly, this story is not alone. Given all of the atrocities happening around the globe (both human-made and nature-made), and the likelihood that climate change and proxy wars will only increase the number of people seeking refuge across borders, this story and the refugee crisis has global relevance.

We don't have to be dealing with Nazi Germany or large scale refugee crises to find the relevance in this story either.

Every single day, all of us are asked to make decisions of conscience in our lives. Our decisions may seem very trivial compared to the ones made by asylum officers or Nazi officers. The situations we're dealing with may not be life or death. But in the end, the stakes of living a life of *Integrity* are always high.

Maybe we're being asked to speak up on behalf of someone who doesn't have a voice. It could be a person, a child, an animal, a bee or an endangered tree.

Maybe we're being asked to defend someone who is being attacked emotionally or physically, or to be honest with a loved one who might strongly disagree with what we have to say. Or maybe we're being challenged to bring attention to a shadow that's showing up in a spiritual community or educational program we're involved in. Or maybe we're having to say 'no' when everyone expects us to say 'yes,' or 'yes' when others expect us to say 'no.'

In all of these cases, we're being asked to trust in our own inner *Authority*. We're being asked to do or say something that might feel risky, that might be judged. We're being given an opportunity to act from a place of *Courageous Self-Trust* … or not.

In the end, I've come to believe it matters less where we engage or apply our *Courageous Self-Trust*. What matters more is THAT we engage it, and that we engage it full-heartedly. Not out of guilt, obligation, fear or unprocessed rage, but out of a genuine and authentic deeper-than-the-mind impulse to honor who we are, to recognize our body and heart's wisdom, and to stay awake to what our conscience tells us in each passing moment.

When we align our *Courageous Self-Trust* with a deep desire to be of service, we unleash the power and intelligence of an invisible network, linking all of us together in ways far more effective and synergistic than we could ever comprehend or plan with our intellects. When we surrender to the currents and impulses of our own hearts, we often find that people, projects, good causes and movements that seemed totally separate at one time, suddenly join together and cross-pollinate to make a larger and more holistic impact.

I also believe (especially during times when we are particularly vulnerable to feelings of despair and resignation) that there is incredible transformative power in standing by and close to anyone we consider to be a true role model. For me, a true role model is someone who embodies the courage, stamina, faith, vision, practicality, perseverance, honesty, self-awareness, compassion, resilience, love and wisdom that are required during these challenging times we're living in. Someone who's 'all in,' whose got their eye on the long game.

The role model who has come to us for the collective is the *Wisdom Keeper* of *Authority* and *Valor*. Let's keep him close in the days and months ahead!

PRACTICAL INVITATIONS TO EXPLORE MORE DEEPLY

Feel free to write your responses down in your journal. If other questions arise for you, answer them too—or instead. Trust yourself. These are just prompts to get you started.

QUESTIONS FOR CONTEMPLATION

When and where in your life have you felt controlled?

Have you felt controlled by specific people? (e.g., a parent, partner, sibling, teacher, etc.) Have you felt controlled by a group of people? (e.g., a community, culture, religion, etc.) Or by a circumstance? (e.g., a trauma, poverty, celebrity, violence, a financial downturn, a polluted environment, etc.) Take time to remember how feeling and being controlled felt in your body, in your heart. How did it impact your thinking, your attitudes about yourself and others and your world view? How did it ultimately influence your behavior? Did you become overly submissive? Or did you become reactive and rebellious? Perhaps different scenarios brought out different responses in you.

Is there an area in your current life where you feel controlled?

A relationship, environment or circumstance that leaves you feeling like you have no other choice than to submit, give in or to rebel? How long would you say you've felt this way? What are the things that you've already tried in order to regain your sense of autonomy and sovereignty? What have you not yet tried? What is the biggest fear or concern that keeps you from embodying more *Courageous Self-Trust* in relation to this situation in your life? If you were to ask the *Wisdom Keeper* of *Authority* and *Valor* for guidance around your current situation, what might he suggest that you do? Or stop doing? Think of one small yet courageous step you could take towards greater *Self-Trust*. Take it!

Are there any ways in which *the fear of being controlled* may actually be running—or ruining—your life?

Perhaps you've found a way to experience a great deal of personal freedom. But you've done so at the expense of intimacy, support or a sense of belonging. What would you say are the biggest prices you've paid to secure your autonomy and freedom?

Have you ever been perceived as, or accused of being, controlling?

Think back to that situation, that relationship. Be as honest with yourself as possible. (Self-trust can only truly develop when we are honest with ourselves.) Can you find a kernel of truth in the accusation or perception? When you are controlling, what does it tend to look like? Does it look like a subtle, unconscious form of manipulation? Does it look like an attempt to take care of people, to rescue or fix a situation? Does it manifest more as anxiety, as a means of allaying a fear? Or as perfectionism, a means of proving your adequacy?

Have you become so afraid of being controlling and misusing your power that you're not using it at all?

Think of a time that you felt a strong inner impulse to stand for something that mattered to you or to speak out, but you didn't because you feared being (at least perceived as) power-hungry, oppressive or abusive. What do you now wish you had been able to do or say then? What did you learn from that situation?

Think back to a few of your best, most cherished relationships. Was there something about those relationships that helped you feel safe enough to surrender, to let go, relax and receive?

Was there something about them that made it easier for you to own your *Authority*, to trust yourself and to speak your mind and heart? What was it about these people—or the quality of your interactions—that helped bring out your flexibility? Your truth? Your *Courageous Self-Trust*? How can you cultivate these qualities in your current relationships so that more people can experience their own *Courageous Self-Trust* in your presence?

WHO INSPIRES *COURAGEOUS SELF-TRUST* IN YOUR PERSONAL WISDOM WHEEL?

Now it's time for you to choose the *Wisdom Keeper* who will sit in your **Wisdom Wheel**, in the position of *Courageous Self-Trust*.

I encourage you to choose this card with eyes closed, and allow the powers of synchronicity to work for you … unless you have a very strong feeling that there is a particular *Wisdom Keeper* who needs to be in this position. If that's the case, go for it!

Spread your cards out face down. You can shuffle them first if you like. These are big cards, so you may have to be creative in how you shuffle. Make sure you have your journal close by.

Before you pick your card, close your eyes.

Resting one or both hands on your heart. Inside, or out loud, in your own words, ask for the right *Wisdom Keeper* to come to you.

Say something like, "I am calling upon you, *Wisdom Keeper*, to hold the space for *Courageous Self-Trust*. I welcome you and trust that you are exactly the *Wisdom Keeper* I need to teach me how to feel, receive and practice self-trust in my life, and to show courage in all of my relationships."

Then reach down with your hand, and either feel the cards … or hold your hand above the cards, and feel the energy of the cards.

Let one call you, and pick that one.

Once you have your card, place it FACE UP at the top of your Wheel, the seat meant for the *Wisdom Keeper* of *Courageous Self-Trust*.

PRACTICAL INVITATIONS TO EXPLORE MORE DEEPLY

NOTE: If you decided to leave the *Wisdom Keeper* of *Authority* and *Valor* in your deck, and you've pulled it for your **Personal Wheel of Integrity**, this likely means that—when it comes to *Courageous Self-Trust*—the personal and collective are especially interconnected for you these days. I encourage you to already begin to notice how the people around you are embodying a sense of inner *Authority* and *Valor*, or NOT doing so. And ask yourself, how might what's going on in the collective be mirroring something going on inside of you?

If you've drawn a different *Wisdom Keeper* than the one I pulled, find the *Wisdom Keeper* of *Authority* and *Valor* in your deck (#21), and place this card right next to the *Wisdom Keeper* you pulled for the seat of *Courageous Self-Trust* on your **Personal Wheel of Integrity**. Allow these two *Wisdom Keepers* to hold the archetype of *Courageous Self-Trust*, *Authority* and *Valor* together. In your contemplations, conversations and journaling, I invite you to let your own imagination help you uncover possible areas of thematic synergy between the two. Enjoy paradoxes where you find them!

GET TO KNOW YOUR PERSONAL WISDOM KEEPER OF
COURAGEOUS SELF-TRUST

Before you look in the Inner Guidebook, I invite you to spend a little time looking at your *Wisdom Keeper*. If their eyes are open, look into their eyes.

If not, gaze upon the face with a soft gaze and a soft heart.

Allow your eyes to drift around the face, taking in the symbols.

Allow your heart to engage even more deeply with the *Wisdom Keeper*.

Notice how this *Wisdom Keeper* makes you feel.

Now look at the number and the word on the card. Does this number or this word have a special association for you? Regardless of what's in the book? What is it? Just make a note in your mind or in your journal. No need to hold onto it.

QUESTIONS TO EXPLORE

Here are some simple questions for you to explore on your own, to help you connect even more deeply with this *Wisdom Keeper* who has been called to sit in the seat of *Courageous Self-Trust*. Feel free to write your responses down in your journal. If other questions arise for you, answer them too—or instead. Trust yourself. These are just prompts to get you started.

Remember: This is just the beginning of your relationship with this *Wisdom Keeper* sitting in the seat of *Courageous Self-Trust*. Even if you don't fully understand why this *Wisdom Keeper* came to you, or why it picked this particular position on your Wheel, it's the perfect one for you. Its mission will be revealed over time, as long as you stay open to it and engage with an inquiry of the heart.

- How do you experience *Courageous Self-Trust* in this *Wisdom Keeper*?

- If you were to sit down and have a conversation with this *Wisdom Keeper*, how do you think their *Courageous Self-Trust* would be expressed? (e.g.. Through touch? Through words? Through an expression in the eyes? Through sharing knowledge? Through ceremony? Through a physical gift? Through a mantra? Through concrete advice? etc.)

- Is there something about this being that could bring out the *Courageous Self-Trust* in you? If it's possible to describe it, what is that something? Are you willing to allow this 'opening to *Courageous Self-Trust*' to happen? What does this particular kind of *Courageous Self-Trust* feel like … in your heart? Your body? Your breath? Just notice. Jot down any insights that come. Take this subtle feeling out into the world today, and see what happens.

- If this *Wisdom Keeper* had a single, simple message for you about *Courageous Self-Trust*, what would it be? Write it down on your **Integrity Wheel** where your *Wisdom Keeper* sits.

DIVE INTO THE BOOK

Take out your book and find the page that corresponds with your *Wisdom Keeper* at the seat of *Courageous Self-Trust*.

At your own pace, do the following:

1. Read Richard Rudd's quote. Look at the Shadow, Siddhi and Gift words that are connected to this *Wisdom Keeper*, inspired by *The Gene Keys*.

2. Allow your mind to add the word *Integrity* to the mix. Play with these various combinations and allow insights to emerge. (e.g., "The *Integrity* of (Gift)," "(Gift) expressed with *Integrity*," "(Gift) that lacks *Integrity*," "(Shadow) of *Integrity*," "*Integrity* that embraces (Shadow)," "The *Integrity* of (Siddhi)," "(Siddhic quality) without *Integrity*," etc.)

3. Read the story of your *Wisdom Keeper*. Then read the Gift for You Section.

4. Remember, as shared in our Initiation Module, the *Wisdom Keepers* are unique individuals, with their own life experience. Your *Wisdom Keeper* has come to understand the nature of the Gift, Shadow and Siddhi (or spiritual essence) that they carry, in their own way.

5. You don't have to relate to the story of your *Wisdom Keeper* right now. You may relate to certain aspects of it, and not others. This is just one story of how one being came to experience a shadow, embody a gift and connect with a spiritual essence. Your story is yours, equally rich, equally fascinating, equally full of potential.

6. Look through the Questions for Contemplation in the Inner Guidebook. Perhaps one or two will open up a door for you. See whether any of the questions in particular connect you to the theme of *Integrity*.

7. Jot any insights, questions or doodles down in your journal.

8. If you are familiar with *The Gene Keys*, this particular *Wisdom Keeper* may correspond with a Gene Key that you have in your profile. Allow what you know about this Gene Key and its unique placement in your profile to creatively synergize with the themes of Courage, Self-Trust, *Authority*, *Valor* and *Integrity*. See what happens!

SHARE WITH OTHERS

I invite you to share your experience with this *Wisdom Keeper* with a friend, partner or inside of a small group of trusted people. Let your fellow explorer(s) know which *Wisdom Keeper* called you and has taken its place at the seat of *Courageous Self-Trust*. Take turns sharing whichever aspect of your journey you've found most inspiring, challenging or interesting. Share from your journal or simply from your heart.

Make sure that you create a safe space where you and others know that whatever you share will be held confidential, as well as respected. You might want to come up with basic sharing and listening guidelines to be sure that everyone feels safe.

EXERCISE #1:
FLIGHT, FIGHT OR FREEZE

Explore a time when you totally lost touch with your inner *Authority*, when you either fought, fled or froze. Thinking back, what or who helped to regain your connection to your *Courageous Self-Trust*? (e.g., a counselor or teacher, a soul-retrieval journey, deep trauma work, self-care or self-soothing practices, etc.)

Note: When we have a traumatic or re-traumatizing experience, our anxiety can take us beyond our capacity to tolerate what's happening. Our frontal lobe shuts down; we lose perspective; our digestion stops working; we enter a state of heightened arousal, hypervigilance and fear. This triggered state can cause us to try to flee, to freeze, or to fight.

Fighting can be an expression of courage. And sometimes it's necessary. But sometimes, when we've got unworked trauma, we can get stuck in fight mode. We fight when it isn't necessary. We fight when another approach or behavior would be much more effective. We end up perpetuating old conflictual dynamics instead of contributing to healthier, more constructive ones.

Because our bodies aren't able to handle digestion when we're in flight, freeze or fight mode, they have to find a way to switch our digestive systems back on. One effective way to do that is to bring about a system crash, which is often experienced as a form of numbness or depression. Unfortunately, during these times, our frontal lobes aren't working that well either. This means that our thoughts are as un-trustworthy now as they were at the height of our trigger.

One of the most important things we can do is to get good at noticing when a state of overstimulation is coming on. If we can catch it before we've gotten to the point where we can't tolerate what's happening, we can remind ourselves to go into self-soothing mode. During these times, it's all about providing ourselves with comfort and relaxation, to give ourselves the experience of being held—either by ourselves or another.

EXERCISE #2:
LEARNING TO READ THE SIGNS

How does your body let you know you're heading into 'controlling mode?' Think of a particular physical sensation that you've come to associate with your need to be in control. Perhaps it's a tightened chest, a rapid heart rate, a clenched jaw, raised shoulders, a nervous tick or a ball in your solar plexus. Whatever it is, get really good at recognizing this sensation. Whenever it arises, gently remind yourself to take one to three deep breaths. Be sure to send your breath into the part of your body where your controlling impulse resides. Try this breath now, with yourself or a partner. Feel your body relax as much as possible on the exhale.

EXERCISE #3:
LETTING OTHERS IN

I bet that your *Courageous Self-Trust* muscles are stronger and suppler now than they used to be! Take a moment to acknowledge how this is true. Acknowledge to yourself or to another that you are now ready to safely receive more intimacy and support than ever before. Think of two simple but concrete ways you can open up to a deeper level of interconnectedness:

In relation to (a person) _____, one way I can open up to more intimacy is by…

_____.

In relation to (a group, my family, a community) _____, one way I can allow myself to

experience more belonging is by _____.

EXERCISE #4:
A *SELF-TRUST* TALISMAN

Find a Self-Trust Talisman to wear. You may have something already that immediately comes to mind. Or, you may want to go on a walk out in nature or through a favorite shop and allow your talisman to find you. Share your Self-Trust Talisman with your partner or group.

EXERCISE #5:
HONOR YOUR *COURAGEOUS SELF-TRUST* INSPIRATIONS

Create an altar or collage in honor of the people who are inspiring embodiments of *Courageous Self-Trust*. These might be people you know who've been particularly true to their nature, who've bravely followed their intuition, or who've spoken out on behalf of their conscience while keeping their *Loving-Kindness* and *Healthy Self-Respect* intact. If there is a particular person, group or organization that especially inspires you, consider supporting them with your time, energy, skills, patronage or donations.

Inspiration Shout-Out: Universal Love Alliance (ULA)

For me, the people of Universal Love Alliance, the human rights organization in Uganda I've spoken of in an earlier module, are some of my most inspiring role models in the *Courageous Self-Trust* department.

Instead of judging, defending themselves or attacking those who don't understand or agree with them (those who literally attack them), they courageously reach out, build bridges, listen carefully and confront empathically. Their love is fierce. Their mission is universally relevant. They are more committed to being of service than to being right.

Instead of constantly fantasizing about leaving their country (like I've been known to do!) in order to avoid the corruption, violence and ignorance all around them (or to escape their own understandable suffering and hardships), they ask what they can do to make their country better, what they can do to serve, protect and give a voice to people who have been marginalized and oppressed.

Instead of turning away from 'bad news,' (in order to avoid uncomfortable feelings or remain untainted by things of an 'unspiritual' nature), they turn towards what is happening. They are not afraid to look at and face the world as it is, even when it is often painful, frightening, utterly disappointing and unjust. More often than not, when they look out at the world and connect with people, they are able to find someone or something to love.

Many on the ULA team themselves have been victims of violence, brutality and discrimination. (Not to mention poverty.) And somehow, they still manage to keep their hearts and minds open to all people, even those who judge them, attack them and wish them harm.

Anyone who can do that, I want to learn from and support. I figure; if they can do it in Uganda with little to no resources, we can do it here.

EXERCISE #6:
WHERE DO I NEED MORE COURAGEOUS SELF-TRUST?

Think of an area in your life where you feel called to embody more *Courageous Self-Trust*. Where (or with whom) have you tended to shrink and second-guess yourself instead of expand and express yourself fully?

Start by writing a list of all of the things you fear might happen if you do what you feel called to do.

_____   _____   _____   _____

_____   _____   _____   _____

_____   _____   _____   _____

_____   _____   _____   _____

Now let your Conscience speak. Through a quick and easy stream-of-consciousness writing process, let your Conscience (not you) fill in the following blanks:

I am (your name) _____'s Conscience. (e.g., "I am Rosy's Conscience.")

I see that (your name) _____ needs to be more courageous and self-trusting, especially when it comes to (describe the situation)… _____.

What upsets or concerns me most about this situation is…

_____.

Given (your name) _____'s (gifts) _____, (skills) _____, and
(areas of wisdom) _____, I believe (your name) _____ is
uniquely able to meet this challenge and make a positive difference.

Of all of the things (your name) _____ might do or say, this is most important:

_____.

I know that (your name) _____ can trust that they are being guided to take action by their loving heart
and wisest self (as opposed to their distorted fears or misguided ego) because…

_____.

In order to be true to themselves and to me, I want (your name) _____ to be willing to risk…

_____.

The *Wisdom Keeper* of *Valor* and *Authority*, like me, wants (your name) _____ to know…

_____.

MODULE FIVE

"And the day came when the risk to remain tight in a bud was more painful than the risk it took to blossom."

~ Anais Nin

WISDOM KEEPING WORDS

Marilee Aronson, PsyD
Clinical Psychologist, Sattva Yoga Teacher, Vedic Astrology Devotee

"I think truly being in one's integrity means being able to bear witness…

Bearing witness to life in all of its magnificence, mystery and pain.

Bearing witness to the depth of our own experience and to the truth of another's.

Bearing witness with clear eyes, an open heart, a steady mind and a courageous spirit."

WHAT IS *REVERENT SURRENDER?*
AND WHY IS IT NECESSARY TO *INTEGRITY?*

Welcome to our fifth module and our final seat in the **Wisdom Wheel of Integrity**. We have arrived at one of my favorite themes: *Reverent Surrender*. As we explored earlier, *Loving-Kindness* and *Healthy Self-Respect* create a sacred balance. Without *Loving-Kindness*, *Healthy Self-Respect* can manifest as coldness, even meanness. Without *Healthy Self-Respect*, however, an abundance of *Loving-Kindness* can turn into unhealthy codependency, martyrdom and people-pleasing.

The quality of *Reverent Surrender* comes to bring balance to the quality of *Courageous Self-Trust*. As we learned in our last module, to be true to our nature and our conscience, and to make an authentic and meaningful contribution to this world, we often need to be brave. We need to be brave enough to break out of the confines of our conditioning, brave enough to speak out against injustice, and brave enough to stand for something that matters deeply to us—even if it doesn't seem to matter to anyone else.

We also need to trust ourselves. We need to know how to stay centered and connected to something deep within us, no matter what's going on around us. We need to stay connected to something entirely unique within us that is simultaneously connected to the whole of existence.

The possibility of changing our world can only exist in Fantasy Land if we don't have self-trust and courage. And, as we learned in our last module, if all we know is how to conform, adapt and follow orders, we're doomed to perpetuate some of the very worst aspects of our nature, and our world.

At the same time, if we have an unwavering conviction that we know what the world needs, and we're constantly imposing our 'good will' on the world around us, if we don't also know how to stop, slow down, listen and surrender to what is (not just how we wish things could be), our *Courageous Self-Trust* goes unchecked. When unchecked, it can become compulsive, dense, forceful and unyielding. Ultimately, it can mask a subtle arrogance towards Life itself.

This final seat on our **Wisdom Wheel** is here to remind us of the power, wisdom and intelligence of Life itself. It's here to humble us, to remind us of just how small we are in the vast scheme of things, and just how little we actually know. This seat is not about trusting ourselves; it's about trusting Life, the great unfolding Mystery.

I can't help but think of the first astronauts who were able to see our earth while standing on the surface of the moon. For the first time, they could see our home from thousands of miles away. A glorious blue pearl floating in the vast ocean of space. Interestingly, it took a whole lot of *Courageous Self-Trust* for these explorers to get to a place where they could surrender to such an expansive state of being, and such a profoundly existential recognition. It's actually a beautiful example of these two polarities joining together in service of each other, and of the kind of *Integrity* we're exploring together.

It is in the spirit of balance that I now call upon the *Wisdom Keeper* who will sit at the base of our **Collective Wheel**, and will make their home in the seat of *Reverent Surrender*.

Let's see who comes to us!

"Justice that love gives is a surrender, justice that law gives is a punishment."

~ Mahatma Gandhi

WHO SITS IN THE COLLECTIVE SEAT OF
REVERENT SURRENDER?

"Patience is about Trust … If you trust in life, you will trust life in every moment, even the challenging moments, and in so doing you will always remain in the flow."

~ Richard Rudd

Gift: *Patience*
Shadow: *Impatience*
Siddhi: *Timelessness*

The *Wisdom Keeper* I pulled on behalf of the collective, the *Wisdom Keeper* who shall be sitting in the seat of *Reverent Surrender* over the coming days and weeks, is the *Wisdom Keeper* of *Patience* and *Timelessness*, with the Shadow of *Impatience*.

How perfect!

So, let me start by sharing the story of this *Wisdom Keeper* with you, and then their Gift to You. After that, I'll share some reflections that came up for me in relation to this *Wisdom Keeper*, and some ways for you to explore your own inner response to the collective *Integrity* themes inherent in this *Wisdom Keeper*'s story.

Get a cup of tea and relax at your favorite reading spot. Ask your heart and soul to open up to receiving the wisdom, power and healing offered to you by this dear friend and ally.

MY WISDOM STORY

When I was a young man, I was always in a hurry. My breath was shallow, and my nerves were on edge. No matter how things seemed on the outside, I always felt that something was wrong on the inside. I owned a small grocery store but had my sights on something bigger. I believed that if I didn't make things happen, they wouldn't. My destiny was all up to me. Time was running out, and I was failing.

There were times when I was so impatient and desperate for my business to grow that I became very pushy. So pushy that my staff quit, suppliers refused to work with me and customers stopped coming. In my despair, I became consumed with pessimism, believing nothing would ever work out for me, no matter how hard I tried. But then one evening, when I was sitting alone and wondering whether I should give it all up, a kind old man knocked on the gate. He held the Book of Changes in one hand, and a tiny tree in the other—so beautiful it glowed. I let him in, and the two of us sat down together and talked for hours. I lost track of all time. Next thing I knew, I agreed to become his apprentice and learn the sacred arts of I Ching divination and Penjing (Chinese Bonsai).

That was many years ago. Now I can laugh as I acknowledge just how much patience it took me to learn *Patience.* How many times my master had to remind me to slow down, breathe deeply and accept whatever was happening in my life. There was no need to manipulate, conquer or collapse. He taught me to treasure nature, flow with the seasons, and that a similar, perfect and orderly rhythm lived and moved in my own soul. Yin would always turn to yang, and yang would always return to yin. *Patience* paid off. My teacher and the trees taught me to trust in life, to honor each moment, even the hardest, most painful ones. Now my life is simple, and I often enjoy the most delicious states of *Timelessness.*

MY GIFT TO YOU

It is time to soften your shoulders and relax your breath. Get quiet. Listen to your own heartbeat. There is nothing you have to do right now. Life is deeply intelligent. Its timing is impeccable; it always knows what's best for you. And you, my friend, are an intricate part of Life, forever-connected to everyone and everything around you. I am here to remind you that nothing happens by accident or without a potential gift. A delayed train can lead to an unexpected encounter. A personal crisis can birth a healing opportunity. An individual's pain can unleash collective transformation. And all with perfect timing. So, take another deep breath, step out of the way and befriend *Patience*. Your Soul will thank you for it.

REFLECTIONS

In the early stages of this *Wisdom Keeper*'s life, he is extremely focused on his own personal progress. He wants to get ahead, make money and become a successful businessperson in the eyes of the conditioning world around him. Constantly running against the clock, he is impatient with himself and others. He's also very hard on himself, which makes him critical and pushy at first, and then cynical and depressed later.

This young *Wisdom Keeper* is not alone. So many of us feel plagued by ticking clocks. Whether the clocks are personal, professional, spiritual or biological, we're afraid of running out of time. We're afraid of missing out on once-in-a-lifetime opportunities, of our lives flying by us, and our having nothing—or no one—to show for it.

Many of us get particularly caught up in the trap of comparing our lives to the lives of others. Given the 'highlight and celebrity culture' that pervades most online platforms, we usually compare our worst moments to other people's best moments—often captured in snazzy snapshots and viral videos. No wonder we feel like we can never keep up, like we'll never make it.

At some point, however, most people who are involved in some sort of spiritual or self-development journey wake up and realize that they want to do more than serve themselves, get ahead or impress people on Instagram. They want to make a difference in the world. They want to be of service.

In the case of this *Wisdom Keeper*, (although this level of detail isn't included in his story), I could easily imagine him transitioning into a time of life when giving meaningful, transformative I Ching Divination readings became more important to him than making a lot of money through his business. I can also imagine how easy it would be for the very same ambition and *Impatience* that made him miserable as a grocery store owner to creep into his service work.

As a Divination Reader, his questions and worries might be different, but the underlying issues would be the same: Is he giving good enough Readings? Are his Readings resonating enough with his clients or making a big enough difference in their lives? Is he reaching enough people? Is his service work growing fast enough? Is he missing out on opportunities to share the wisdom he's gained over the years? Should he go into teaching or public speaking so he can reach even more people? You get the idea.

Since Service and Sacred Activism are central themes we've been exploring together, let's take a moment to look at the shadow of *Impatience* in the context of our service work.

If I've learned anything over the years, it's that if we want systemic change—not surface change—we're going to need to be very *very* patient. The systems, structures, institutions and conditioning forces that currently run our planet are the manifestation of layers upon layers of unworked through, paradoxical, sticky and complicated collective wounding … which has made its way into the inner psyches and distorted behavior patterns of highly unique individuals. Most problems we face as Sacred Activists have been around for a long time. A nice chunk of them will likely hang around far after we're gone.

This means that we're going to need to acquire an important skill: the ability to rejoice in each incremental step we take. We need to get *really* good at seeing progress—even when it seems minuscule or is completely invisible to most people. We also have to remember that sometimes a sign of true progress can look a whole lot like a hot mess!

I have a dear friend and mentor based in San Francisco named Armand Volkas. He is a psychotherapist, drama therapist and theater director who has been working with a powerful theatrical tool called Playback Theatre, in collaboration with one of his legacy projects, Healing the Wounds of History.

> If you're interested, here's a link (**TINYURL.COM/LIVING-ARTS**) to a few videos my husband Kim took of his Playback Theatre ensemble reflecting a few of the *Wisdom Keepers* and their stories.

Back to Armand. He's traveled the world over many times and has received international acclaim for creatively bringing together groups of people who have been traumatized by long histories of conflict. He's brought Chinese and Koreans together, Germans and Jews, Armenians and Turks, Palestinians and Israelis. The list is endless. One of the core understandings of his work is that *there is a victim in every persecutor, and there is a potential persecutor in every victim.*

We are all human beings—shadow and all. Our ability to heal the wounds of history is dependent on our willingness to courageously explore, feel and own the entirety of our own humanity. It also depends on our willingness to walk in another's shoes, even in the shoes of a person or group of people whom we've directly experienced (or learned to perceive) as our enemy.

Ram Dass—a man whose teachings have influenced me greatly—used to talk about how spending two weeks with his parents was all the spiritual teaching he needed. (Likely more effective than a year of yoga in India!) I bet some of you can relate. I know I can!

One moment, I'm looking out at the world and observing all sorts of people doing unkind and unconscious things. I find myself wondering why people can't "just be more self-aware, balanced and loving." And then the next moment, (literally sometimes, the very next moment!), I'm in a room or on the phone with a family member, and I'm acting like a lunatic.

We're all 'works in progress.' We all have our hypocritical moments. Most of us are walking contradictions. None of us have this perfection thing down. Even some of the great spiritual masters who've been considered awakened have been known to reveal some less-than-ideal traits and do some damage.

A nice dose of humility seems to be called for on all fronts. It doesn't matter who we are, how educated we are, how old we are, how many hours on a therapy couch or meditation cushion we've racked up, how many spiritual workshops we've attended, how many impressive degrees or certificates we've amassed, or how many books, films and brilliant programs we've created, or inspirational speaking gigs we've 'totally rocked.'

The better we get at acknowledging our own contradictions, and loving ourselves regardless, the better we get at being with—and working to inspire change in—everyone. That's the bottom line.

If you agree that cultivating *Patience* is a worthy goal, I encourage you to remember that the very best way to go about it is to be willing to have an abundance of experiences in your life where you don't get what you want exactly when you want it. Or you just don't get it.

Practice makes perfect! One of the best places to start, as this *Wisdom Keeper* so beautifully models for us, is to work on cultivating *Patience* towards our *Impatience*. Everything gets easier from there.

Let's now turn our gaze towards a beloved cousin of *Patience*, and a word that lives in this particular seat on the **Wisdom Wheel**: *Reverence*.

Patience and *Reverence* are connected, but they are not the same.

Several years ago, a lovely woman, writer and teacher named Eileen Pardini asked me to share some words about *Reverence* for her online magazine. I'll share a bit of what I wrote here with you because it feels relevant (not just Reverent!).

A FEW WORDS ON REVERENCE

There are places in our lives where *Reverence* comes easy. Who wouldn't take a look at a sleeping child, for example, or a gorgeous flower, or a golden sunset, and not experience at least a moment of heart-opening, breath-taking and awe-inspiring appreciation?

There are also those other places, like when we're spending time with relatives who aren't necessarily withholding their opinions or spreading the love. Or when we're interacting (and sharing the planet) with people whose worldviews, values and behaviors are so different from our own. Or when we're looking in the mirror at our own gloriously, imperfectly human reflection.

The same goes when we're engaged in a creative process (like fulfilling our life's purpose!), and things aren't going quite as smoothly, quickly or neatly as our minds would like. During times like these, it can be so hard to practice the kind of joyful presence, respect and gratitude for life so beautifully captured by the gift of *Reverence*.

Sometimes, when we're feeling impatient with our life and the way it's going, when *Reverence* is beyond our reach, it can help to start with Mindfulness—the ability to be with and witness our uncomfortable experience from a place of calm, neutral presence. We relax, breathe deeply. We watch our thoughts without grasping or pushing away. We do our best to loosen the hold of judgments, agendas and time pressure. We practice *Loving-Kindness* towards ourselves.

When I'm in one of my "My life purpose can't unfold fast enough!" states, I like to pull out my *Gene Keys* book and read one of my favorite passages by Richard Rudd, about the Gift of *Restraint*:

"To begin anything, you must first have a clear intention. The more selfless your intention, the more power it will have. If you begin with the right intention, then everything will follow, but you must resist the temptation to interfere with the process out of fear. The intention is the seed, and the seed contains all the necessary ingredients and properties that will be needed in the journey ahead. The seed even contains the specific fragrances that will attract the right allies at the right times.

It is also true to say that the greater the power, the longer it takes to germinate. The seed of a yew tree and the seed of a sunflower are similar in size. However, whilst the sunflower will grow to its full size within the space of a few months, the yew tree has depth and complexity and will begin at a different pace and follow its own timing. It may take 10 years just to reach the height of the sunflower, but it may live as long as 5,000 years. So it is with all human ideas and actions … We humans cannot see the details of the journey ahead; we have to trust in the direction that our intention takes, even if it does not make sense to us at the time. This is the power of Restraint—to allow your life to unfold without urgent demand."

Gosh, I just love that passage from *The Gene Keys*. The Gift of "***allowing our lives to unfold without urgent demand***."

Just take that in. Ahhh…

It reminds me of another favorite line from the Course in Miracles: *"Those who trust can afford to be patient."*

Take a moment to imagine yourself looking upon your own life—your own soul's journey, with its ups and downs, ins and outs, steps forward and steps backward. Imagine yourself looking upon it with the same *Reverence* and trust you'd give a yew tree.

What would your life be and feel like if you had a profound and genuine *Reverence* for the natural timing of your own growth process? If you ***really*** got out of the way, if you ***really*** gave yourself permission to sit back and watch—not just with calm neutrality, but in wonder and awe—at the pure intelligence guiding each and every (visible and invisible) step of your unfoldment.

Just for a moment, breathe into that possibility. Notice what happens in your body when you do.

THE OTHER SIDE OF THE REVERENCE COIN

Of course, as often happens, when we really drop in, when we truly let go of pushing, forcing and controlling life's natural unfoldment, we realize that there's another (in some ways paradoxical) aspect to *Reverence*. It's one that asks us **not** to wait.

Anais Nin wrote one of my all-time favorite quotes: *"And the day came when the risk to remain tight in a bud was more painful than the risk it took to blossom."*

This quote touches on this other side of the *Reverence* coin. Just as there are times when we need to sit back, relax and practice trust-infused *Restraint*, there are other times in our lives when a seed is actually ready to sprout. There are times when something within us is authentically chomping at the bit, ripe enough to poke itself out of the soil and dance around in the sunlight.

During times like these, some of us stand in resistance to this inner growth impulse. We make the mistake of being—or at least seeming to be—**too** patient. But the truth is that we're not being patient. We're being afraid. We're afraid of not being ready … of not being good enough. We're afraid of failing out loud. Some of us can be just as afraid of being 'too good' or having too much success. We can understandably fear having to deal with the expectations, pressures, idealizations and envy that can come as a result of 'positive visibility.'

Often, these kinds of fears cloak themselves in procrastination and paralyzing perfectionism, both shadow expressions of *Patience*.

In the end, when we're stuck in a procrastinating or perfectionistic rut, we're doing the opposite of practicing *Reverence*. We're *refusing* to show *Reverence* towards the emergent within us.

We're also refusing to *Surrender* to our soul's genuine impulse to share our gifts, love and creativity with the world, and to bloom more fully.

So, as is often the case, we're looking at a paradox, or a balancing act. Sometimes *Reverent Surrender* asks us to slow down, sit back and surrender to what is, without doing or changing a thing. Other times, *Reverent Surrender* asks us to *surrender to our gifts* and their readiness to be shared—even if our minds don't think we're ready, or good enough, or able to handle the consequences of coming out of the closet, whether we view the closet as 'positive' or 'negative.'

Either way, *Reverent Surrender* requires that we open up to the probability that our own growth and blooming process is mysteriously—synchronistically—connected to the growth of the Universal garden.

This seat on the **Wisdom Wheel** is ultimately Taoist in nature. It's all about surrendering to 'the Way.' It's about embracing the impersonal, mysterious, ever-changing, indescribable, all-encompassing, always-in-motion, nondual, dynamic ground of being. It's about acknowledging that we live inside of a universe—that we ARE a universe—that is intrinsically alive. Where yin and yang, dark and light and 'female' and 'male' need each other equally, where they play and dance together, ebbing and flowing into a perfected balance.

Taoism reminds us that we need not 'do anything' … ever. Instead, 'doing' can simply happen through us, through spontaneous action. Taoists call this kind of spontaneous action I'm talking about 'action through non-action,' or 'Non-Action.'

Non-Action is not the same as doing nothing. It's referring to a kind of action that is not driven or caused by rational thinking or cultural conditioning. It is not exaggerated, wasteful or superfluous. It's not even courageous, or 'self'-trusting, in the way we usually think about those concepts. Instead, Non-Action (or 'action through non-action') arises naturally out of a simple, humble, compassionate, grace-filled inner attunement to the Way. There is no 'self' involved really.

This is why it's so perfect that this seat sits opposite to—and in balance with—*Courageous Self-Trust*, which at least on one level, is very much about having an authentic, healthy *self* and acting on its impulses and inner knowing.

In the context of *Integrity, Reverent Surrender* invites us to explore what 'doing by non-doing' (*Wu wei*) actually feels like in our everyday lives, and in our service work.

Mahatma Gandhi, a true *Wisdom Keeper* and Sacred Activist of our times, was an Indian lawyer, anti-colonial nationalist and political ethicist. He played an enormous role in liberating India from British Rule, and he did so using nonviolent resistance. For decades, his life and courageous actions have inspired civil rights movements around the world. And while he wasn't a Taoist, there are many parallels between his philosophy, way of living and being an activist, and what we're exploring together here.

Gandhi made us aware of how we (human beings) tend to react to violence with more violence. He understood that aggressive actions caused disruptive impacts on the world around us. The more forceful (thus disruptive) our actions, the harder it becomes to find gentle alternatives and elegant solutions to our shared problems.

He dedicated his life to finding—and demonstrating—an alternative to knee-jerk reactivity. He referred to the methods of Nonviolent Resistance that he modeled and implemented as 'Satyagraha,' or 'Insistence on Truth.' In life (and in death), Gandhi showed us what it means to master the art of graciously circumventing forcefulness, violence and defensiveness, even in the presence of fear and life-threatening (in his case life-ending) danger.

For Gandhi, Satyagraha was a 'love-force' or 'soul-force' that required tremendous compassion. It also required *Patience*. He knew that being cruel to a perceived enemy, or attempting to beat or scare the Truth into them, never works. It may feel good in the moment, but it only makes things worse in the long run. It causes excess disturbances in the field, limits our ability to find more kind and efficient alternatives, contributes to the piling up of unhealed wounds, and adds to the complexity of the relational frequency field. It also increases the intensity and experience of divisiveness, thus dualist ways of perceiving and thinking.

Gandhi saw *Patience* as a form of necessary suffering for the Sacred Activist. For the ultimate Truth to come out or be vindicated (like the truth of every person's dignity, worthiness and sovereignty), sacred activists have to be willing to slow down and 'wait' for a genuine opening of hearts and minds of others in order to have the deepest and longest-lasting impact.

This doesn't mean that activists are supposed to sit around and do nothing. Gandhi certainly didn't do that! But it does mean that we need to practice a certain amount of *Reverent Surrender*, of Non-Action. It means that we don't continually force our will on the world, even if we're certain it's good will. It means that we need to viscerally understand, accept and respect that a genuine transformation of attitude and perspective in people takes time.

For a moment, just think back to some of the deepest changes you've made in your own life, and how different you are now from who you were just five years ago, ten years ago, twenty years ago. It takes time to truly change a world view, to understand who we are, to grasp why we're here, to come to terms with what really matters. We're all still evolving. I find it helpful to remember that when I get impatient, or have a hard time understanding people, or why the world is in the state it's in.

"Be the change you wish to see in the world."

That is one of Gandhi's most famous quotes.

It reminds us that if we truly want to create a more peaceful world, and I don't think any of us would be participating in this class if that weren't the case, we must cultivate a certain amount of peace within us, no matter what is going on around us. In order to 'be that change,' Gandhi made the ultimate sacrifice. His life.

It feels right to bring our reflections on this final seat on our **Wisdom Wheel** to a close by honoring Gandhi—a human being who struck such a profound balance between *Courageous Self-Trust* and *Reverent Surrender*.

PRACTICAL INVITATIONS TO EXPLORE MORE DEEPLY

Feel free to write your responses down in your journal. If other questions arise for you, answer them too—or instead. Trust yourself. These are just prompts to get you started.

QUESTIONS FOR CONTEMPLATION

Where in your life—and with whom (including yourself)—are you feeling most impatient? How does your *Impatience* show up? Is it through:

- a constantly nagging Superego in your mind

- jittery sensations in your body

- rushing from one thing to the next without stopping for a break

- constantly checking your screen of choice to see who's contacted you or what's next on the agenda

- filling 'space' with people, technology, entertainment, activities

- constantly focusing on the future

- measuring success through your accomplishments

- judging yourself incessantly for not being good enough, not having gotten far enough, quickly enough

- an experience of not being fully present

Pay special attention to your body in the coming hours and days. Come to recognize the sensation of *Impatience*. See if you can practice breathing patiently into that sensation without expecting it to change or transform in any way. Just patiently be with it.

Now think of an aspect of our world that you struggle with the most. What is it that you continually lose *Patience* with? Is it:

- Discrimination in the form of Racism? Sexism? Heterosexism? Classism? Ableism? Ageism? Anti-Semitism? Islamophobia? etc.

- The refugee crisis?

- Continual war?

- The misused power of pharmaceutical companies?

- The banking industry, the military-industrial complex?

- The politicized news, the bias of the media?

- The continually decreasing amount of funds available for true investigative journalism or alternative perspectives?

- Corporate greed or influence over government decision-making bodies?

- The multi-faceted and deep-seated results of colonialism and slavery around the globe?

- The massive amounts of waste, toxins and disrespect being unleashed on our earth?

- The denial of our responsibility to treat our earth (and all of its inhabitants) more lovingly, regardless of one's stance on Climate Change?

- A general diminishment or ridiculing attitude towards 'all things spiritual' in mainstream society?

- The ways in which otherwise good ideas, values and movements are distorted, usurped, used and politicized for bad purposes?

- Nationalism, tribalism, or humanity's seeming inability to rise above divisive 'us vs. them' thinking?

- All of the ways people are hypocritical and lacking self-awareness and self-responsibility? Is it rampant hypocrisy—the way people judge and punish others for what they do themselves?

- How easy people are in general to manipulate, how easy it is to get people to act from a place of fear, not love?

- That so many of the best, kindest, most generous people are struggling to survive or fund their humanitarian efforts, while some of the seeming 'worst' people are steeped in money and power, and using their abundant resources to ensure they don't lose them?

I could go on and on. What matters most is that you locate that aspect of the human and world condition that gets under your skin. That aspect that, despite your highest intentions, makes it hard to sleep at night, makes it nearly impossible for you to listen to people with different perspectives, gets you into unproductive conflicts, and shuts your heart down.

Once you've identified this issue, create an image of it in your mind's eye. Then see or sense it shrink to the size of a pea, sitting right in front of you. Then imagine yourself slowly rising above the space where you are, keeping your eye on the pea … until you can no longer see it. As you continue to rise, allow yourself to see more and more of the Earth. Imagine you are an astronaut gazing upon the blue pearl of our planet from thousands of miles away.

From this vantage point, you know that this 'pea of a problem' exists. You know that it is somewhere on the planet. Now feel and see the planet moving through space and time, rotating on its axis, circling around the sun … As you see or sense this image, allow your breath to relax. See if you can give yourself just a bit of time where all you're doing is witnessing, breathing, with gentle awareness … Do this five minutes every day for a week, and see what happens.

If you fully trusted in Life's perfect timing, and that nothing happens accidentally, how might your thoughts, feelings, attitudes and relationships change? What might you do—or not do—differently?

Come up with three examples of when something seemingly horrible happened, and then something wonderful, useful or meaningful came out of it. One example in your personal life, one in the personal life of someone you care about, and one in the world. How did your initial conclusion in each situation change as the story continued to unfold?

Remember the last time you experienced a sense of *Timelessness*. Where were you? What environments and activities (or non-activities) tend to bring out this ability in you to experience a sense of *Timelessness*?

Mountains? Bodies of water? Open meadows? Vast vistas? Meditating? Yoga? Art-making? Listening to certain kinds of music? Pick one or two of these that speak to you (and that are possible) to focus on. Spend a little more time than usual connecting to *Timelessness* in the coming days.

If you could show *yourself Patience* today (in your personal journal, with a friend, in a small group, in your everyday life), what would you do?

What needs to happen inside of your own body, breath and thinking mind for you to actually feel *Timelessness*?

Are you willing to make a pact with yourself that just for today, you are going to BE more ... and hurry (and worry!) less?

If you experience an uncomfortable feeling, tell yourself, "I'm embracing this feeling for the sake of all of humanity."

WHO INSPIRES *REVERENT SURRENDER* IN YOUR PERSONAL WISDOM WHEEL?

Now it's time for you to choose the *Wisdom Keeper* who will sit in your **Wisdom Wheel**, in the position of *Reverent Surrender*.

I encourage you to choose this card with eyes closed, and allow the powers of synchronicity to work for you … unless you have a very strong feeling that there is a particular *Wisdom Keeper* who needs to be in this position. If that's the case, go for it!

Spread your cards out face down. You can shuffle them first if you like. These are big cards, so you may have to be creative in how you shuffle. Make sure you have your journal close by.

Before you pick your card, close your eyes.

Resting one or both hands on your heart. Inside, or out loud, in your own words, ask for the right *Wisdom Keeper* to come to you.

Say something like, "I am calling upon you, *Wisdom Keeper*, to hold the space for *Reverent Surrender*. I welcome you and trust that you are exactly the *Wisdom Keeper* I need to teach me how to feel, receive and practice *Reverent Surrender* in my life and in my relationships."

Then reach down with your hand, and either feel the cards … or hold your hand above the cards, and feel the energy of the cards.

Let one call you, and pick that one.

Once you have your card, place it FACE UP at the very bottom of your Wheel, the seat meant for the *Wisdom Keeper* of *Reverent Surrender*.

PRACTICAL INVITATIONS TO EXPLORE MORE DEEPLY

NOTE: If you decided to leave the *Wisdom Keeper* of *Patience* and *Timelessness* in your deck, and you've pulled it for your **Personal Wheel of Integrity**, this likely means that—when it comes to the quality of *Patience*—the personal and collective are especially interconnected for you these days. I encourage you to already begin to notice how the people around you are embodying *Patience*, or NOT doing so. And ask yourself, how might what's going on in the collective be mirroring something going on inside of you?

If you've drawn a different *Wisdom Keeper* than the one I pulled, find the *Wisdom Keeper* of *Patience* and *Timelessness* in your deck, and place this card right next to the *Wisdom Keeper* you pulled for the seat of *Reverent Surrender* on your **Personal Wheel of Integrity**. Allow these two *Wisdom Keepers* to hold the archetype of *Reverence* and *Surrender* together. In your contemplations, conversations and journaling, I invite you to let your own imagination help you uncover possible areas of thematic synergy between the two. Enjoy paradoxes where you find them!

GET TO KNOW YOUR PERSONAL WISDOM KEEPER OF
REVERENT SURRENDER

Before you look in the Inner Guidebook, I invite you to spend a little time looking at your *Wisdom Keeper*. If their eyes are open, look into their eyes.

If not, gaze upon the face with a soft gaze and a soft heart.

Allow your eyes to drift around the face, taking in the symbols.

Allow your heart to engage even more deeply with the *Wisdom Keeper*.

Notice how this *Wisdom Keeper* makes you feel.

Now look at the number and the word on the card. Does this number or this word have a special association for you? Regardless of what's in the book? What is it? Just make a note in your mind or in your journal. No need to hold onto it.

QUESTIONS TO EXPLORE

Here are some simple questions for you to explore on your own, to help you connect even more deeply with this *Wisdom Keeper* who has been called to sit in the seat of *Reverent Surrender*. Feel free to write your responses down in your journal. If other questions arise for you, answer them too—or instead. Trust yourself. These are just prompts to get you started.

Remember: This is just the beginning of your relationship with this *Wisdom Keeper* sitting in the seat of *Reverent Surrender*. Even if you don't fully understand why this *Wisdom Keeper* came to you, or why it picked this particular position on your Wheel, it's the perfect one for you. Its mission will be revealed over time, as long as you stay open to it and engage with an inquiry of the heart.

- How do you experience *Reverence* in this *Wisdom Keeper*? *Surrender*?

- If you were to sit down and have a conversation with this *Wisdom Keeper*, how do you think their *Reverence* or Surrender would be expressed? (e.g., Through touch? Through words? Through an expression in the eyes? Through sharing knowledge? Through ceremony? Through a physical gift? Through a mantra? Through concrete advice? etc.)

- Is there something about this being that could bring out the *Reverence*, or Surrender, in you? If it's possible to describe it, what is that something? Are you willing to allow this 'opening to Surrender' to happen? What does this particular kind of *Reverence* feel like … in your heart? Your body? Your breath? Just notice. Jot down any insights that come. Take this subtle feeling out into the world today, and see what happens.

- If this *Wisdom Keeper* had a single, simple message for you about *Reverent Surrender*, what would it be? Write it down on your **Integrity Wheel** where your *Wisdom Keeper* sits.

DIVE INTO THE BOOK

Take out your book and find the page that corresponds with your *Wisdom Keeper* at the seat of *Reverent Surrender*.

At your own pace, do the following:

1. Read Richard Rudd's quote. Look at the Shadow, Siddhi and Gift words that are connected to this *Wisdom Keeper*, inspired by *The Gene Keys*.

2. Allow your mind to add the word *Integrity* to the mix. Play with these various combinations and allow insights to emerge. (e.g., "The *Integrity* of *Patience*," "*Patience* expressed with *Integrity*," "*Patience* that lacks *Integrity*," "Impatient *Integrity*," "*Integrity* that embraces *Impatience*," "The *Integrity* of *Timelessness*," "*Timelessness* without *Integrity*," etc.

3. Read the story of your *Wisdom Keeper*. Then read the Gift for You Section.

4. Remember, as shared in our Initiation Module, the *Wisdom Keepers* are unique individuals, with their own life experience. Your *Wisdom Keeper* has come to understand the nature of the Gift, Shadow and Siddhi (or spiritual essence) that they carry, in their own way.

5. You don't have to relate to the story of your *Wisdom Keeper* right now. You may relate to certain aspects of it, and not others. This is just one story of how one being came to experience a shadow, embody a gift and connect with a spiritual essence. Your story is yours, equally rich, equally fascinating, equally full of potential.

6. Look through the Questions for Contemplation in the Inner Guidebook. Perhaps one or two will open up a door for you. See whether any of the questions in particular connect you to the theme of *Integrity*.

7. Jot any insights, questions or doodles down in your journal.

8. If you are familiar with *The Gene Keys*, this particular *Wisdom Keeper* may correspond with a Gene Key that you have in your profile. Allow what you know about this Gene Key and its unique placement in your profile to creatively synergize with the themes of *Patience, Impatience, Reverence*, etc. See what happens!

SHARE WITH OTHERS

I invite you to share your experience with this *Wisdom Keeper* with a friend, partner or inside of a small group of trusted people. Let your fellow explorer(s) know which *Wisdom Keeper* called you and has taken its place at the seat of *Reverent Surrender*. Take turns sharing whichever aspect of your journey you've found most inspiring, challenging or interesting. Share from your journal or simply from your heart.

Make sure that you create a safe space where you and others know that whatever you share will be held confidential, as well as respected. You might want to come up with basic sharing and listening guidelines to be sure that everyone feels safe.

EXERCISE #1 & 2:
TRANSCENDENCE AND IMMINENCE

Back in 1999, I was an expressive arts therapy student at the California Institute of Integral Studies in San Francisco, California. One of my professors, Jack Weller, shared about a fascinating scientific experiment on meditation. My memory is a bit hazy, so I mostly remember the gist of the experiment, which I'll share with you now.

Each subject of this particular experiment was a master of meditation. One subject came from a 'transcendent' tradition. His meditation method involved the discipline of focusing on a single mantra over a long period of time. The other subject came from an 'imminent' tradition. His practice involved being radically present to whatever was happening in each moment, internally and externally. You could say it was closer to a mindfulness tradition.

Each of the subjects were hooked up to a sophisticated device designed to measure brain activity as well as various bodily systems (e.g., heart, nervous, digestive, endocrine, circulatory, respiratory, muscular, etc.).

The subjects were then asked to begin meditating in the manner they were accustomed. The first subject focused his attention intently on a sacred mantra. The second practiced his usual radical presence. A control group (not practitioners of meditation) was asked to simply sit silently during the experiment.

While the two practitioners meditated, and the control group sat in silence, the experimenters did something interesting. They made a series of sudden, loud, banging sounds. They did this for a long time and not according to a particular rhythm. While they did this, they carefully watched the ways in which the bodies of the two meditators and the control participants responded to the noises.

At first, the bodies of both meditators responded in exactly the same way, with a degree of shock and strong physiological reactivity. But then, slowly, their responses began to diverge in a way that was quite profound. The transcendental meditator's body reacted less and less to each loud sound, until his body showed no reactivity at all.

The imminent meditator's body, on the other hand, continued to react to each loud sound as if it were the very first time. There was absolutely no decrease in physiological responsiveness, no matter how many times the meditator was exposed to the sound.

The control participants became increasingly desensitized to the sounds over time, but were never able to fully transcend the shock or avoid a physical reaction.

In a way, you could say that the transcendent meditator literally *transcended* the experiences of the body. With each repeat of the mantra, his consciousness expanded and expanded until there was no experience of the small self, or ego, or body. He ultimately reached a state where there was no physical discomfort, no experience of disruption, no disturbance in his personal energetic field—just peace, calm and total freedom from the 'illusion of the Maya.' There was no separation between him, his body, the sound and the Great Oneness.

The imminent meditator had an equally powerful yet in some ways opposite experience. It didn't matter how many times he heard the same sound; he never got used to it. He and his body remained radically open to his environment—breath by breath, minute by minute, hour by hour. In a way, his mastery of 'radical presence' and 'beginner's mind' trained him to *transcend the experience of desensitization* experienced by the control group.

Both meditators showed a great deal of mastery. Both demonstrated core stability. Both attained a state of freedom. Both practiced true presence. And in a way, both experienced a profound Oneness with *all that is*.

This fascinating experiment comparing the two paths of imminence and transcendence is also showing us two kinds of *Patience*, or trust.

There's the kind of *Patience* we experience when we're able to transcend this body, this life—when we can see it all as a game and 'rise above' like the astronauts seeing the earth for the first time from thousands of miles away. There's a visceral openness and relaxation that takes place when we're able to experience our little body and personality's infinitely insignificant role in the Great Cosmos, when our expanded awareness allows us to surrender our small self-identity to our soul identity, to the 'Oversoul,' and ultimately to *all that is* and can't be named.

But there is also a kind of Patient *Surrender* that comes from learning how to be fully present in this body, this incarnation—breath by breath, moment by moment. This kind of *Patience* requires that we surrender to a deep vulnerability that we open ourselves up completely to our inner and outer environments. We don't try to transcend discomfort (even if our knowing minds may understand that all discomfort is ultimately an illusion). We welcome each and every one of our emotional and visceral experiences without pushing away, clinging or freezing.

The Practical Invitation:

Now I'd like to invite you to do two meditation experiments, with the aim of exploring and embodying different aspects of *Patience, Timelessness, Reverence* and *Surrender*. Be open to what you discover.

Meditation #1: Transcendence
- For 10 – 20 minutes, choose something to focus on. It might be a mantra, the flame of a candle, a single affirmation that you repeat, the count of beads on a mala, or the decision to count a predetermined number of breaths and then start counting again, etc. No matter where your mind goes, return to that single focus.

Meditation #2: Radical Presence
- For the same amount of time you used in Meditation #1, stay radically present to each moment, each rising physical sensation, each sound in your environment, each thought wafting through your mind, etc. Notice and feel all of it, to the best of your abilities, without pushing away or grasping what you're noticing and feeling.

EXERCISE #3: COMIC RELIEF

One of the advantages of having a teenager in the house is getting introduced to very silly TV shows that one might not have otherwise discovered. My daughter Maya got me to watch a show called "New Girl," and there's one episode in that show that is my all-time favorite. It involves one of the main characters, a young man named Nick.

The Scene: Nick is sitting on a park bench, feeling utterly grumpy and upset, and an older man walks over and sits next to him. At first, Nick is totally annoyed at the man and tries to get the man to leave him alone. The man looks at Nick with such unconditional love and kindness that Nick can't help but pour his heart— and mind—out, until he experiences a total release. This particular character (later known as Tran) never speaks. At first, it's not entirely clear that he speaks English at all. But he comes back in later episodes, always playing the wise, loving friend who is magically able to relax Nick's monkey mind and open his heart.

There's something about the relationship between Nick and Tran that I don't only find hilarious, but touching. I just love watching a wise old man holding space for a young person who is struggling, whose mind is tearing his life apart with questions, doubts, emotional turmoil and complexities. Tran is a *Wisdom Keeper*. Even though he's on a sitcom, he embodies a kind of *Reverent Surrender* that is contagious and worth watching. Here's a clip I hope you enjoy as much as I do!

TINYURL.COM/TRAN-ZEN

EXERCISE #4:
REVERENCE PRACTICE—A THREE-FOLD INVITATION

This is a chance to practice *Reverence* towards yourself, and your own (creative/life) process, especially during times when it feels especially difficult:

Start with a little intention seed check-up

Pick an intention that you'd like to focus on. It might be to clean your closet, write a book, create a work of art, organize an event, plant a garden or something else. Whatever it is, make sure it feels meaningful to you.

Now, whatever intention you're working with, make sure that there's a good chunk of love at the core of your seed. See if there's a way you can make it less about you, (e.g., whether you're good enough or not), and more about the people or beings you just might help if you get out of your own way and share what you feel moved to offer. (Remember, it's not about being perfect!)

Embrace your inner yew tree

Remind yourself, as often as you need to, that as long as you're planting seeds that have been sincerely sprinkled with love, there is an intelligence at work, in you, and all around you. This intelligence is permeating every situation, guiding, gathering and patiently setting the pace behind the scenes. It is creating just the right conditions for your full and glorious unfoldment. Trust that this is happening, whether you know it or not, understand it or not, or feel like you have any control over it or not.

Then take a deep breath and let go. (Who knows? Your little seed might be growing something entirely different than you imagine, yet something equally magnificent. Seeds can be delightfully tricky that way!)

Chances are, you'll know when it's time to take a risk and bloom, because you won't be able *not* to (even if you're scared). Your right time will have arrived, and your whole being will be primed to meet it.

A BLESSING IN DISGUISE (CHINESE FOLK STORY) AS RETOLD BY DR. YANG, JWING-MING

Republished with permission of YMAA Publication Center®
https://ymaa.com/articles/stories-proverbs/blessing-in-disguise

A long, long time ago, there was a kind old man who lived on the plains outside the Great Wall of China. The gentle old man had only two passions in his life: collecting rare breeds of horses, and his son, whom he loved more than anything else.

The old man and his son would ride their horses every day. They would travel great distances to trade horses, meet new people, and enjoy the good fortune that life had bestowed upon them.

One morning, a servant left the stable door open and one of the old man's favorite stallions escaped. When the neighbors heard the news of the stallion's escape, they came to comfort the old man. They told him they were sorry he had had such bad luck.

But strangely enough, the gentle old man was not upset. He explained to his neighbors that losing the horse wasn't necessarily bad luck. There was no way to predict that the horse would escape, it just happened, and now there was nothing that could be done about it. "There is no reason to be upset," said the old man. The neighbors soon realized that there was nothing they could do to help get the horse back, and that they shouldn't feel sad for the old man's misfortune.

One week later, the stallion came back, and he brought with him a mare. This was not just any mare, but a rare and valuable white mare. When the neighbors heard of the old man's good luck, they quickly came to congratulate him. But again, the old man was not excited. As he had explained before, it was not necessarily good luck that had brought him this new and beautiful white horse. It just happened, and there was no reason to get excited over it. Still a bit puzzled, the neighbors left as quickly as they had come.

A short time later, while his son was riding the white horse, she slipped and fell. She landed on the son's leg, and broke his leg, so that he would always walk with a limp. Again, the neighbors came to the old man's house to give their sympathy for the bad luck that had befallen his son. One of the neighbors suggested that the old man sell the mare before any more bad luck could happen, and others said that he should take his revenge and kill the mare. However, the old man did neither. He explained to the neighbors that they should not feel sorrow for his son nor anger towards the mare. It was purely an accident that could not be predicted, and there was nothing he nor they could do to change it. At this point, the neighbors thought the old man was crazy and decided to leave him alone.

Two years later, an enemy invaded the country, and all of the old man's neighbors were drafted to defend the country against the attack. Because the old man's son was lame, he did not have to join in the fighting. The war was very bad, and most of the old man's neighbors were killed, but his son was spared because he had been hurt by the white horse two years earlier.

Very often, when an event takes place that everybody thinks is good luck, the end results are disastrous. In the same way, an unlucky event can bring about happiness. Therefore, you should not lose your will to continue if an unlucky event happens, nor should you be too overjoyed or feel too self-satisfied because of a lucky event, or because something that you desire comes very easily to you.

FINAL MODULE

*"We may have all come on different ships,
but we're in the same boat now."*

~ Martin Luther King Jr.

Now that we've made it to the end of our **Wisdom Wheel**, let's take some time to review where we've been … so we can appreciate the full journey we've been on.

We began with our Initiation Module, where you had the chance to learn about the story behind the *Wisdom Keepers*, how they came to be, and to receive an introduction to your own deck.

During our Initiation, I shared how I've come to hold the *Wisdom Keepers* as a loving—and diverse—family of wise beings that we can turn to for support. I shared how having wise beings around us is more important now than ever, since we're living in a time when so many of us have lost touch with the ways of our ancestors and indigenous wisdom traditions. Lastly, I shared some words about the Wheel, its sacred and universal significance, and why it's such a fitting container for an exploration on *Integrity*.

Then we all got our **Wisdom Wheels** ready for the journey. Each of you had the chance to choose (with your eyes open) the *Wisdom Keeper* who is meant to sit at the very heart of your **Personal Wisdom Wheel**.

After you had a chance to connect with your own *Wisdom Keeper*, I pulled the *Wisdom Keeper of Imagination and Illumination*, with the shadow of *Confusion*, to sit at the heart of our **Collective Wheel**. Initiating our collective journey, she encouraged us to bless our pain and *Confusion* with the gift of our awareness and creativity, as well as to set our imagination free—to begin the sacred process of dreaming the world we want into being.

Our next Module was devoted to exploring the theme of *Loving-Kindness* and the essential role it plays in the cultivation of *Integrity*. We looked at how sometimes, in our attempts to be honest, to speak our truth, and to do the right thing, we forget to be kind. Not only towards others, but towards ourselves—especially when we expect ourselves to live up to impossibly high standards. In the spirit of a resilient heart, I called upon a *Wisdom Keeper* to sit in the seat of *Loving-Kindness* on our **Collective Wheel of Integrity**: the *Wisdom Keeper of Equality and Tenderness*, with the shadow of *Weakness*.

This *Wisdom Keeper* encouraged us to embrace those parts of ourselves that have been forced into—or have found a home in—the proverbial closet. Those parts of us that for whatever reason have felt forbidden, charged, controversial or just plain unsafe to acknowledge, embrace or express. Together we learned that if humanity is going to develop *Integrity* together, we need to embrace those parts of us that we've learned to reject. We're also going to be kind to the people around us who look, feel, think and act differently from us. If we are to uncover what true *Equality* looks and **feels** like, we're going to need a certain amount of *Tenderness* and humility. We're going to need to learn how to listen and to have honest-yet-kind conversations, where everyone gets to be human, make mistakes, and be in a process of learning and growth.

Our next Module was all about *Healthy Self-Respect*. When we have *Healthy Self-Respect*, we can set healthy boundaries, care for ourselves, and get much better at caring for others. We looked at the **Wisdom Wheel of Integrity** as a system of checks and balances. Each council member on the Wheel contributes to the overall balance of the whole. We need all of these *Wisdom Keepers* … equally.

Just as a strong moral code—without *Loving-Kindness*—can end up looking and feeling a lot like meanness, *Loving-Kindness*—without *Healthy Self-Respect*—can end up looking and feeling a lot like unhealthy people-pleasing, self-sacrifice and codependence. During our Module of *Healthy Self-Respect*, we acknowledged how *Loving-Kindness* junkies (like myself) get into trouble when our deep desire for peace is driven by an even deeper fear of conflict—and anger. The bottom line is that being a 'good person' isn't always enough to make a positive difference in our lives or in the world.

The *Wisdom Keeper* who came to sit in our **Collective Wheel's** seat of *Healthy Self-Respect* was the *Wisdom Keeper of Resolve and Divine Will*, with its shadow of *Exhaustion*. This *Wisdom Keeper* reminded us that sometimes—even though our minds are overwhelmed with all of the work there is to do—we need to relax. To *really* relax.

For those of us who tend to lose ourselves in care-taking and social change engagement, it is crucial that we learn how to balance our desire to serve the world and our need to enjoy our lives. Otherwise, we're just going to burn out. And the world has enough burned-out healers and grumpy activists.

This *Wisdom Keeper* encouraged us to stand our ground, learn how to set healthy boundaries and be generous with ourselves. He reminded us that sometimes saying 'no' to the right thing can be more powerful than saying 'yes,' and that self-care is essential to the cultivation of *Integrity*.

I shared a story from my own life as a sacred activist, and how deeply I've needed (and continue to need) to be reminded of this important life lesson. I also shared how this lesson can be a painful and humbling one; since it confronts us with the reality that sometimes very bad things happen to very good people, and sometimes there's very little we can do about it.

In our next Module, we explored the essential theme of *Courageous Self-Trust* and how it relates to *Integrity*. Together we looked at what happens when we don't sufficiently develop this essential quality, and how without it, very good people can end up doing very bad things. We looked at how difficult it can be in today's overstimulating world to find our center. We explored how many of us are constantly exposed to competing pressures—telling us what to think, feel, need, value and do. I shared some about Human Design, a fascinating system that uniquely explores what it means to live in alignment with one's own unique '*Authority*' or truth compass. When integrated into an everyday practice, Human Design (or Gene Keys-infused Integral Human Design) can significantly contribute to people's experience of authenticity, self-trust and right timing.

In the end, if we learn to open our hearts to life, we don't need a system to guide us. We just naturally orient ourselves towards our highest potential. And when we do this, our decision-making process can only serve Creation—since we are an integral part of it.

The *Wisdom Keeper* who came to sit in our Collective Seat of *Courageous Self-Trust* was the *Wisdom Keeper of Authority and Valor*, with its shadow of *Control*. This trust fund baby's journey showed us how at first, *Courageous Self-Trust* often shows up as a rebellion against conditioning forces, as a big NO. But eventually, it manifests through a deep, compassionate and service-oriented inner YES.

In this Module, I shared about the Milgram Experiment and what can happen when we haven't sufficiently worked our *Courageous Self-Trust* muscles. This experiment shows how vulnerable we can become to manipulation and control, and how if we're not careful, we can end up doing things that go against our conscience, simply because we don't have the courage or inner strength to resist.

A good example of this is taking place at the Southern border of the U.S., where a new government policy is forcing Asylum officers to do things that go against their conscience. I shared about a man named Doug Stevens who stands out as an inspiring role model of *Courageous Self-Trust*. These days, we need as many brave, compassionate and self-trusting role models as we can get. Every day we are provided with opportunities to stand for something or someone we care about and to live in alignment with our hearts, our conscience and our *Integrity*.

In our last Module, we met the *Wisdom Keepers* meant to sit at our final seat in the **Wisdom Wheel of Integrity**—the seat of *Reverent Surrender*. Just as *Healthy Self-Respect* creates a sacred balance with *Loving-Kindness*, the quality *Reverent Surrender* comes to bring balance to *Courageous Self-Trust*. We remembered that if we're all too sure of what the world needs, if we never slow down enough to listen, honor and surrender to what is, our *Courageous Self-Trust* can end up looking a lot like an arrogance towards Life. Our intended service can become energetic bullying.

Reverent Surrender is here to help us trust in the naturally unfolding intelligence of the Universe and to surrender to a relaxed state of humility.

The *Wisdom Keeper* who came to sit in our Collective Seat of *Reverent Surrender* was the *Wisdom Keeper of Patience and Timelessness*, with the Shadow of *Impatience*. His journey took him from a place of stressful, hurried desire to get ahead as a businessperson, to one of deep relaxation, trust, and the desire to be of service.

In our reflections, we turned our attention to the shadow of *Impatience* in the context of service work. We reminded ourselves that systemic change takes a LOT of time, and that if we truly aim to heal historical wounds and transform collective conditioning, we're going to need a lot of *Patience*. We're also going to need to cultivate the ability to notice and celebrate each small triumph, realizing that sometimes progress is difficult to see at first, or downright messy!

I shared about the powerful, bridge-building project called Healing the Wounds of History, led by my dear friend and mentor, Armand Volkas. This international experiment in empathy emphasizes the healing and transformative power of 'walking in another's shoes'—even a perceived enemy's shoes. I shared about Ram Dass, another *Wisdom Keeper* who has modeled humility and *Patience* throughout his life, not to mention a good dose of humor. He reminded us that most of us on the spiritual path—no matter how impressive or enlightened we may seem on the outside—are works-in-progress. And that's OK. In fact, finding a way to embrace ourselves—contradictions and all—is essential if we want to make this world a better place.

We explored how one of the best ways to learn and practice the art of *Patience* is by not getting what we want when we want it. As our *Wisdom Keeper* modeled for us, cultivating *Patience* towards our *Impatience* is one of the best places to start!

Then we turned our gaze towards *Patience*'s cousin, *Reverence*. I shared from an article I wrote on *Reverence*, which included one of my favorite passages from *The Gene Keys* book by Richard Rudd, about the Gift of *Restraint*, the beauty of "allowing our lives to unfold without urgent demand," and the importance of having a clear loving intention at the onset of any endeavor. We imagined what it would be like to look upon our own lives with the same kind of *Reverence, Patience* and trust we'd give a yew tree.

We also took a look at a common shadow that can emerge. Sometimes, we hide our fears of success and failure behind the guises of *Reverence* and *Patience*. When we do this, our shadow manifests through procrastination, perfectionism, and ironically, the refusal to *Surrender* to our soul's desire and readiness to share its love and gifts with the world.

We then turned our attention to the essentially Taoist nature of this particular seat on our **Wisdom Wheel**. We explored what it means to Surrender to 'the Way'—to 'do through not doing.' We ended this Module with one of the great *Wisdom Keepers* and Sacred Activists of our time, Mahatma Gandhi. Gandhi saw *Patience* as a form of necessary suffering for the Sacred Activist. He taught and modeled how sacred activists, dedicated to the practice of Non-Violent Resistance, must sometimes be willing to slow down and 'wait' for a genuine opening of hearts and minds of others, in order to have the deepest and longest-lasting impact. He understood that continually forcing our will on the world, even if we're certain it's good will, doesn't work.

We ended our last Module with an invitation to think back upon our own life's journey, to honor how far we've come, as well as *all that it took* to get to be where we are today. Deep change takes time.

As our *Wisdom Keepers* have shown us, deep change also requires an ability to embrace paradox.

HOLDING PARADOX

A while back, I stumbled into an old conversation between Ram Dass and Terence McKenna, as a part of McKenna's "Prague Gnosis" Dialogue Series, which took place in 1992, in Prague, Czech Republic, during the International Transpersonal Conference.

Terence McKenna was an American ethnobotanist, mystic, 'psychonaut,' author and dedicated student of shamanism who advocated for the responsible use of naturally occurring psychedelic plants. Referred to as the "Timothy Leary of the '90s," he also came up with a concept about the nature of time based on fractal patterns he discovered in the *I Ching*, which he called novelty theory. So in a way, his life's work is a wonderful reminder of the *Wisdom Keeper* who came to sit in our collective seat of *Reverent Surrender*!

I so enjoyed witnessing these two compassionate mystics talk about the importance of embracing paradox, and how challenging it can be to see the beauty and perfection of each moment, while remaining deeply sensitive to the pain and suffering in the world. Both realities are true simultaneously. Without compassion, the love of beauty and perfection becomes a heartless bypass. But without an ability to see and trust in the natural unfoldment of *all that is*, we can drive ourselves insane in an attempt to push the river of life upstream.

As we look at our **Wisdom Wheel**, we see how *Integrity* is all about balance. It's about learning how to hold and work with paradox.

- We have so much darkness. And yet, there is much Light.

- We have so much pain, and yet, so many opportunities to practice compassion.

- We have free will. And yet, we have no choice.

- We have our true nature. And yet, we're always under the influence.

- We are genetic beings. And yet, our genes are surprisingly responsive to our own thoughts and attitudes.

- We can choose to practice abundant self-care. And yet, we live in environments that are abundantly full of pollutants, chemicals and toxins, and it's beyond our control.

- We can get sick from drinking polluted water, breathing toxic air and eat genetically-enhanced foods.

- And yet, Near Death Experiencers tell us that the true cause of illness is Fear and Stress, and that the frequency of Love can heal even the most diseased bodies. Researchers like Masaru Emoto, the author of The Hidden Messages in Water, similarly provide evidence for the healing and transformative power of loving thoughts.

As we bring our time together to a close, I want you to think of your **Wisdom Wheel** as a gentle invitation to whirl like a Divine Dervish who isn't afraid to get a little Dirty.

Integrity, like Life itself, is a dance. When you are centered in your *Integrity*, there is no part of the human dance floor that is off limits to you. Every corner, nook and cranny of the space in which you find yourself becomes sacred.

INTEGRITY TAKES A VILLAGE

The other day, I was in a car with a couple of lovely co-housing neighbors, on our way to the Upaya Center, a meditation center in Santa Fe, New Mexico founded by Joan Halifax Roshi. One of the women was talking about how alone she'd been feeling, how deeply she longed for more people in her life who shared her devotion to Spirit and desire to make our world a more loving place. She then said something that I'd like to share with you now, as we bring our experience together to a close. She said, "I'm always talking about how I want to live in *Integrity*. But how can I do that if I'm all alone?" I was so touched by her words, and the truth in them. At first, the process of coming into our *Integrity* is an inside job. If we aren't sufficiently balanced within, if we haven't gotten to a place where we can embrace a certain amount of paradox, we're likely to bring unhealthy and distorted versions of ourselves into our interactions with others, further exacerbating the imbalances in the world around us. However, once we've cultivated a conscious and caring enough relationship with *Loving-Kindness*, *Healthy Self-Respect*, *Courageous Self-Trust* and *Reverent Surrender*, we need to engage with others, to learn what it means to collaborate with *Integrity*.

- If we're all alone, there's no one to be kind to.

- If we're all alone, we have no opportunities to learn how to set healthy limits.

- If we're all alone, we have no one to teach us how to care for and respect ourselves.

- If we're all alone, we have no one to take courageous leaps with, no movements to join, no collaborators to encourage us to be brave or to support us when we feel afraid.

- If we believe we're all alone, we're missing out on the greatest truth: separation is an illusion and that we are, have always been and will always be deeply connected to *all that is*.

Our planet ultimately depends on groups of unique yet aligned people coming together to serve, heal, innovate, build and transform!

If you feel particularly drawn to group work, there is a fascinating *Gene Keys* experiment (or game) that I can highly recommend. It's called the Delta Program. For a period of seven weeks, seven people come together to embark on a transformative adventure. Each week, in service of the 'group soul,' each member is invited to contemplate and embody a particular Life Focus: 1) Purification of the Mundane, 2) Relational Healing, 3) Emotional Peace, 4) Transparency in the Heart, 5) Selflessness in Speech, 6) Harmony in Thinking, and 7) Attunement to Spirit. By the end of the seven weeks, everyone has taken a journey through each life arena, and the whole group takes an evolutionary leap! Google, "Delta Program, the Gene Keys" to learn more!

ONE MORE WISDOM KEEPER
TO TAKE WITH YOU ON YOUR JOURNEY!

The secret of the Gift of Integrity is to be able to hold your own space without reacting to your judgments or self-judgments.

~ Richard Rudd

Gift: *Integrity*
Shadow: *Judgment*
Siddhi: *Perfection*

MY WISDOM STORY

From a young age, I knew something was wrong with the way women were treated in my society. My father talked down to my mother, and she let him. Then she'd fret and complain behind his back. But she never spoke up for herself, and encouraged the same sense of *inferiority* in me.

In my teens, I became angry. I saw her life as sad and pathetic, and promised myself I'd never be an oppressed woman. So I rejected all things 'mother.' I spoke my mind, broke the rules and took on the world. I became an independent, staunch feminist, refusing to be patronized. It got to a point where my father threatened to disown me. My mother tried to calm the waters, but deep down she felt ashamed of her unruly daughter.

I left the country and built a new life as an activist and artist. When my parents visited, I'd watch my father condescend, and my mother make nice. I felt *superior* to both of them, either rolling my eyes or flying off the handle. I didn't realize just how victimized I felt by my mother's victimization until I was invited to a friend's house to meet her parents. Like mine, they came from a traditional background. The father dominated the conversation. The mother nodded and smiled. But somehow, my friend was still able to enjoy them and herself. Her kindness, and her acceptance of their limitations, brought out the best in them.

I began to *judge myself* for having judged my mother so harshly, and for not seeing how similar to my father I'd become. Despite all we'd put her through, my mother kept treating us with respect and gentleness, never losing her temper. For the first time in my life, I saw the strength in her vulnerability. Though she could still benefit from standing up for herself, she had a capacity for compassion and compromise that I desperately needed. Thanks to her, I've devoted my life to helping people understand and work through their childhoods, so they can open their hearts and live with *Integrity*.

MY GIFT TO YOU

I am here to help you complete your childhood. It takes courage to uncover the wounds from your past. As you release yourself from the messages and modeling that no longer serve you, you will be free to see and receive the gifts from your parents, with a soft, compassionate heart. When you are truly in your *Integrity*, it won't be possible to take the *judgments* of others personally, or to identify as a victim—of yourself or anyone else. This is not a path to be walked alone, so reach out for support. Allow a friend, therapist, mentor or spiritual counselor to accompany you as you revisit those painful experiences that hardened your heart, made you feel *inferior* or *superior*, or kept you from expressing yourself freely and connecting deeply. Over time, you will learn to judge not from the mind but from the heart.

QUESTIONS FOR CONTEMPLATION

- Where do you tend to feel *inferior*, or *superior*, to others? Who are you being hard on, even if you don't like to admit it?

- Where is self-judgment most alive in your life? Who are you negatively comparing yourself to?

- In what ways does your self-judgment keep you from owning and honoring your own inner authority?

- What does *Integrity* mean to you? Name one thing you can do today to feel more in your *Integrity*.

- How can *Perfection* be an inspiration in your life, rather than a driving force to an unattainable ideal?

BLESSINGS

I wish you all the best as you weave Boldness, Vulnerability, Risk and Relaxation into your life. And remember, even though there will be times when it feels like the world is going down the tubes and there's so little that you can do, *so much can be done through you*—and through your loving, synergistic and creative relationships with others.

Keep your **Wisdom Wheel of Integrity** close by for a while. And even when you feel it's time to dismantle it or put it away, create a mini-version of it that you can keep by your side. Allow it to remind you to:

- Dream the world you want to see with your heart and *Imagination.*

- Embrace *Loving-Kindness* and *Tenderness* towards yourself and others.

- Relax, take good care of yourself and practice *Healthy Self-Respect.*

- Honor your *Authority* and engage in *Courageous Self-Trust.*

- Be deeply *Patient* as you blossom through *Reverent Surrender.*

A FINAL WISDOM KEEPING PRAYER

Evelyn Aronson, My Wise & Wonderful Mother!

"I am **THANKFUL** for another day of life.
I am thankful for all the blessings that life brings to us.
May I make the most of all these blessings.
May I **KNOW** as much as I can,
EXPERIENCE as much as I can,
and **CONTRIBUTE** to the lives of others
so that we can all make the most of this gift of life."

Continue the Journey

DESIGNED TO BLOSSOM

WALKING A FINE LINE

NEXT STEPS!

THE GENE KEYS

WISDOM KEEPERS

IF YOU FEEL INSPIRED TO DIVE DEEPER

THE WISDOM KEEPERS

64 FACES OF REVERENT SURRENDER

EMBODY YOUR PERSONAL & PROFESSIONAL POTENTIAL WITH THE WISDOM KEEPERS
(DECK, BOOKS & ONLINE COURSES)

WISDOMKEEPERS.NET

DESIGNED TO BLOSSOM

A COURSE IN COURAGEOUS SELF-TRUST

BLOOM INTO YOUR AUTHENTIC SELF THROUGH THE DESIGNED TO BLOSSOM
FOUNDATIONAL COURSE AND RESOURCE BOOK IN HUMAN DESIGN
(BOOKS & ONLINE COURSE)

WISDOMKEEPERS.NET/DESIGNED-TO-BLOSSOM-TEACHINGS

WALKING A FINE LINE

A HEALTHY SELF-RESPECT PRACTICE

DEEPEN YOUR INTEGRITY DANCE WITH "WALKING A FINE LINE: HOW TO BE A
PROFESSIONAL WISDOM KEEPER IN THE HEALING ARTS" (BOOK & ONLINE COURSE)

TINYURL.COM/FINE-LINE

THE GENE KEYS

A TRANSMISSION OF LOVING-KINDNESS

UNCOVER YOUR GIFTS BY DIVING INTO THE GENE KEYS
(BOOKS, COURSES & TRAINING PROGRAMS)

GENEKEYS.COM

FEATURED WISDOM KEEPERS

(Wisdom Keepers in the order of appearance)

ERIKA GAGNON

Canadian Artist and Ceremonial Leader

Contact: Erikagagnon11@gmail.com

or on Facebook at **"Erika Gagnon Ceremonial Leader"**

Erika Gagnon is a Canadian ceremonial leader and wisdom keeper of mixed-race ancestry, who has walked the "Camino Rojo / Red Road" for 25 years, working with Indigenous elders of North and South America and their ceremonies, traditions and medicinal plants. She has walked through the altars of the Vision Quest, Sun Dance and Danza de los Epiritus, and has the blessing of her elders to continue their traditions leading Temazcal (sweat lodges), water blessing, tobacco and other healing ceremonies. She also offers personal healing sessions.

MIREYA ALEJO MARCET, M.A., MFT

Psychotherapist, Artist, Breathworker & Sacred Altar Creatrix

Alma Que Canta: A Path with Heart & Soul

ALMAQUECANTA.COM

Mireya Alejo Marcet, M.A. MFT, is an artist, licensed psychotherapist, teacher, professional astrologer and expressive arts therapist. Since 1988, Mireya has been committed to the process of spiritual growth, consciousness exploration and creative expression. Certified by the Grof Transpersonal Training (GTT), she has been a Holotropic Breathwork facilitator since 1993 and has held workshops all over the world.

SHARON KUKUNDA
Teacher & Executive Director of Universal Love Alliance of Uganda
UNIVERSALLOVEALLIANCE.ORG

Sharon is the Associate Director of ULA. She is a teacher by profession and a Ugandan Human Rights Defender who believes in the equal treatment of all human beings, and the inclusion and acceptance of all people regardless of who the person is. She believes in treating others the way she would love to be treated.

VALERIE CREANE, PsyD
Clinical Psychologist & Spiritual Counselor
VALERIECREANE.COM

As a Psychotherapist, Certified Life Coach and Spiritual Director, Valerie's work is profoundly influenced by three streams of experience: depth psychology, coaching and spirituality. Psychology taught her to work deeply with people, respecting the influence of early experiences and relationships; coaching taught her to value action and real-life change; and her spiritual practice has taught her awareness of energy and how to shift energy to mobilize change, as well as the value of surrendering to Spirit in any healing endeavor. Valerie also offers vocational evaluations for individuals seeking greater clarity about their career paths.

KARIN VON DALER, REAT, MPF
Expressive Arts Therapist, Clinical Psychologist, Self-Care Artist
KARINVONDALER.COM

Karin von Daler is a multimodal artist, psychologist, expressive arts therapist and the Creator of *The Self-Healing Oracle Cards*. She has trained and taught internationally and developed the method Creative Mindfulness and the course "The Art of Self-Healing." She is the co-author of several books and is about to release her new online class and cards on self-care and self-healing through creativity, rituals and nature. Karin is in private practice as a therapist and supervisor and lives in Copenhagen. She loves to paint, write, dance and play the harp.

THE WISDOM WHEEL OF INTEGRITY

Mbali Marais
Wisdom Keeper & Traditional Healer
OurDivineMedicine.com

Mbali Creazzo is a global medicine woman trained in the Dagara, West African and South African traditions. She sits on the Council of Crowns of the Mother of the Waters and is a Diviner and voice for the ancestors and teachings of Indigenous Wisdom. A descendant of a Khoi Khoi female healer, as confirmed by Credo Mutwa, Mbali has been accepted as a daughter of the AmaHegebe clan from the Xhosa tradition in rural Eastern Cape. Her Bushman name means 'Purity,' and she carries the essential integrity necessary to guide people to meet with the Sacred Shamans of the Ancient. She is the inspiration behind the best-selling book, *29 Gifts*, by Cami Walker.

Marilee Aronson, PsyD
Clinical Psychologist, Sattva Yoga Teacher, Conscious Traveler & Vedic Astrology Devotee
MarileeAronson.com

Marilee Aronson, PsyD, is a spiritually–oriented licensed clinical psychologist with a wide range of experiences in clinical and community settings. She is passionate about travel and the gifts that come from exposure to different ways of being in the world. She has profound respect for the power of movement, meditation, rhythm, energy work and alternative approaches to healing.

Evelyn Aronson, M.A.
Lifelong Educator, Community Connector & Mother to All
EvelynAronson.com

Evy has had a lifelong passion for making the most of life, this "wonderful gift that we must not take for granted." After attending undergraduate school at Northwestern University, she received her master's degree from the University of Chicago. She taught for over thirty years in diverse educational settings, and was honored with the first Outstanding Teacher of the Year Award from Skokie District 68, in Illinois. More recently, she taught at the Lifelong Learning Institute at National-Louis University and the Beth Emet Institute of Adult Studies.

ADDITIONAL RESOURCES

Learn more about the Delta Program (Gene Keys):
HTTPS://GENEKEYS.COM/DELTA

Learn more about the Karpman Drama Triangle Model:
KARPMANDRAMATRIANGLE.COM

Other Books by Karpman:
Collected Papers in Transactional Analysis (2019)
A Game Free Life (2014)

Book on Codependency Referring to Karpman's Work:
Codependent No More by Melody Beattie

Listen to "The Outcast" podcast, by This American Life:
THISAMERICANLIFE.ORG/688/THE-OUT-CROWD

Watch the Living Arts Theatre Ensemble work with the *Wisdom Keepers*:
TINYURL.COM/LIVING-ARTS

ABOUT THE ARTIST/AUTHOR

Rosy Aronson, Ph.D., is an Artist, Author and Blossoming Guide with a Masters in Expressive Arts Therapy and a Doctorate in Intuitive Listening & the Creative Arts. An avid permission-giver, pressure-dissolver and embracer of the unknown, Rosy believes we are literally designed to blossom, and the more each of us radically trusts, honors and expresses our true nature, the more magic we can create together.

In addition to the *Wisdom Wheel of Integrity Course & Workbook*, Rosy has created the **64 Faces of Awakening**, **The Wisdom Keepers Oracle Deck**, **The Wisdom Keepers Inner Guidebook** and **The 64 Faces of Awakening Coloring Book** to reflect essential healing archetypes that lie at the foundation of our universe.

She has also authored the **Designed to Blossom Foundational Course and Creative Workbook**, the **Designed to Blossom Resource Book**, the **Walking a Fine Line: How to Be a Professional Wisdom Keeper in the Healing Arts** course and book, and **A Tale of Serendipity**. Her deepest intention is to provide empowering tools for people to awaken to their gifts, walk with integrity, and bloom into their authentic selves.

Printed in Great Britain
by Amazon